WHY
Simple
Discipleship

TO HASTEN THE WEDDING

268 Missions   **Kuya Raul**

LIBERTY HILL PUBLISHING

Liberty Hill Publishing
2301 Lucien Way #415
Maitland, FL 32751
407.339.4217
www.libertyhillpublishing.com

Paperback ISBN-13: 978-1-6628-3064-8
Hard Cover ISBN-13: 978-1-6628-3065-5
Ebook ISBN-13: 978-1-6628-3066-2

WHY SIMPLE DISCIPLESHIP
To Hasten The Wedding

I can only give all thanks to God. He not only chose to save me from His wrath but, in His wise and purposeful sovereignty, He also orchestrated and laid the foundation of Simple Discipleship in my life. He gave me disciplers who faithfully poured into me, molded me as clay and *"guided my hand in God"* (2 Kings 16:16). Thankfully, they did not throw up their hands when this clay was stubborn and unyielding much of the time. Thank you: Tim Davy, Bob Noyes, Greg Priebe, Dick Dungan, Dane Robinson, Mark Stortvedt, Ralph Cook, Steve Shank, Pete Payne, David Bendinelli, Bruce Boelter, Russ Doty, James Sharp, Steve Snyder, and Boy Borela.

Along with these godly men to follow, God also gifted and surrounded me with Proverbs 17:17 ironmen to walk and run alongside to sharpen me and strengthen *"my hand in God"* (1 Samuel 23:16). Thank you: Darrin Deichmann, Steve Busskohl, Glenn Wapelhorst, Ted Smith, Ed Wicker, Tim Metcalf, Dave Kruse, Mark Laidman, Sam Miller, Pete Stein, Jim Cooper, John George, Dale Taylor, Mike Durrell, Chris Parsons, Fred Lewin, Bruce Sivil, Mike Applegate, Chuck Longtine, Kirk McCrimmon and Dick Snyder.

For these men and their wives who unselfishly shared their husbands' ear, counsel, and brotherly love, I am sincerely grateful. And I am indebted.

I must mention how grateful I am for the publishers and web-sites who have graciously given their permission to share. Some were very encouraging and even excited to share, understanding that we are called to be a blessing (1 Peter 3:9).

Huge thanks to Runner Francisco, Ezra (*Magic Box Paradigm*) and Bambi Roizen (*Unequally Yoked*), Kirk McCrimmon, Meliza Solan, and Hannah Gross for all your incredible help with your suggestions, questions and editing, even till the early hours of the mornings *"while it was still dark"* (Mark 1:35 ESV) and every normal person was still fast asleep. You probably were thinking it would not be as much as it was. But thank you for enduring it and for always expressing your excitement in doing it.

I have to share this anecdote of my very first edit. My son, Runner was very excited to read and help edit this book for me. But the next day he came and said, *"Dad, if I have to read a sentence in a book several times, I will put it down and not read the book. I know you read old Puritan books which most people do not read. You've also been memorizing books of the Bible. Puritans and Bible authors have mile-long sentences. In your book, your first sentence, Dad!?!? Come on!"* Lol! Well, I had to cut down my sentences. Thank you, Son!

Thank you to my children and the men whom I have had the privilege to disciple through the years. You honour me by thinking you might somehow learn something or even anything from me. I am sure that most of what you have learned is what not to do from my many mistakes.

"So even to old age and grey hairs, O God, do not forsake me, until I proclaim Your might to another generation, Your power to all those to come" (Psalm 71:18 ESV).

May all of you and all those whom you disciple take to all the world what God has shown and taught us about Simple Discipleship. Let us always be mindful that we do all this to hasten the return of Jesus our Bridegroom and The Wedding—the Joy of all joys!

"Three crucial decades in world history. That is all it took. In the years between AD 33 and 64 a new movement was born. In those thirty years it got sufficient growth and credibility to become the largest religion the world has ever seen and to change the lives of hundreds of millions of people. It has spread into every corner of the globe and has more than two billion putative adherents. It has had an indelible impact on civilization, on culture, on education, on medicine, on freedom and of course on the lives of countless people worldwide. And the seedbed for all this, the time with it took decisive root, was in these three decades. It all began with a dozen men and a handful of women: and then the Spirit came!"

Michael Green
Thirty Years That Changed the World[1]

"So much happened in thirty short years! It makes me ask, "What may God do through a modern local group of believers throughout the same period of time?"

Tony Merida
Christ-Centered Exposition Commentary: Exalting Jesus in Acts[2]

WHY SIMPLE DISCIPLESHIP
To Hasten The Wedding

BEGINNING

At the outset, let me be clear that this simple book is not a theological treatise on discipleship. First, because I am not that clever. Second, there are already many good books and online articles on disciple-making. For example: *The Master Plan of Evangelism* by Robert Coleman[3] and *Multiply* by Francis Chan.[4] These men do an exemplary job explaining 1) "what" discipleship is: the simple plan of Jesus to win the world for God. And His simple plan started with the strategy of choosing, calling, and training of only a few ordinary men; and 2) the practicals of "how" to be a disciple and make disciples.

This book will touch upon some of what these authors have already penned for us. I will even quote them and others, as I cannot improve upon what they have said. The main thing I pray that you see in these pages is what I am only beginning to see as the incredibly amazing "fruit" of Simple Discipleship. And how ridiculously simple it is to produce and reproduce! I do not know how I did not see this earlier.

Basically, this is just a small book about my big God, Jesus, and the big things He wants to do through people who are not striving to be big themselves, but God the Father being big in them and His Spirit's power through them to *"turn the world upside down, proclaiming, "There is another King, Jesus!"* (Acts 17:6-7 ESV).

My prayer is that after reading this book, your thought is not, *"What a great book!"* No. I pray you would see that **GOD is great** in this book. This is in obedience to what I believe He told me years ago, to *"not strive to be a great man of God, but rather a man in whom GOD is great!"* And I have endeavored to walk in that with my marriage, my family, our home, my company, and church—that *GOD* be great! For it is all about Him. So, from this simple book, I pray that *"you may have ample cause to glory in Christ Jesus!"* (Philippians 1:26 ESV).

We will touch on the "what" and "how" of discipleship, which is simply Life-on-Life, Person-to-Person passing on knowledge and experience, but we will focus more on "why" Simple Discipleship, hence the title. We must know why. We need a compelling reason why.

Yes, we make disciples firstly because it is what Jesus commanded before He ascended to heaven after His resurrection from the dead (Matthew 28:18-20). We should also be making disciples because discipleship will bear significantly more fruit and substantively richer fruit than the man-made ministry-traditions the Church has been tire-fully employing for so long.

Why Discipleship? More specifically, why Simple Discipleship, which is one-on-one discipleship? Because this is discipleship according to Jesus. These were actually ideas for titles for this book:

Discipleship According to Jesus, Why Simple 1-1 Discipleship, Back to Simple Discipleship, or if I were Jonathan Edwards, *"The Why and the Fruit of Returning Back to Simple 1-1 Life-on-Life Discipleship According to Jesus From His Word, the Bible."*

So, Why Simple Discipleship?
- Jesus modeled it.
- Jesus commands it.
- Simple Discipleship reproduces more fruit.
- Simple Discipleship reproduces richer fruit.
† **Why? To hasten The Wedding—the Joy of all joys!**

We will expound on these throughout the book.

God's commands are commands, not traditions. From His Word, we will see that discipleship is not a man-made tradition or just another church program, but a clear command from God. There is no room for doubt here. We will contrast this simple command of discipleship with the complicated ministry-traditions of men, which sadly produces more exhausted and burnt-out professionals and volunteers. It also seems that more and more exciting things to boost church attendance are constantly being added to a long list of ministry-traditions, which are not bad, but only pack our already full schedules even fuller, taking up every small bit of margin we have left.

The 'All and Only' principle is to do *All* God commands and *Only* what God commands. We will see how the sons of Aaron offered up *"unauthorized fire"* to the Lord (Leviticus 10:1 ESV). And we will see how many ministry-traditions might fall under this category of *"unauthorized fire."*

We will look at the real numbers, sad statistics, and testimonies of volunteers and men who pastor, all of whom are far too busy, consumed with ministry-traditions, and too many burn out as a sad result.

We will show how instead of producing exhaustion and burnout, following Jesus' command of Simple Discipleship will produce significantly more genuine disciples who are transformed, grounded, mature, equipped, and fruitful, without destroying ourselves and our families in the process.

Our Lord Jesus said He will build His Church. What does this mean? It means just that. He will build His Church. He has called us not to the building of His Church or competitive marketing of our churches. He has called us to the mission of going and making disciples.

Finally, and this is what excites me most: the "fruit" of Simple Discipleship is the ultimate and final end and answer to **Why Simple Discipleship**! We will see how *our* generation might easily be *that* generation in Matthew 24:34 that sees the return of Jesus by following His simple command to go and make disciples, not of every person, but of every people group (Matthew 28:19).

But we must awaken His Church's desire for her First Love again, for her to long for her Bridegroom's return and for The Wedding—the Joy of all joys!

I will begin with an abridged version of my story and my experiences with being discipled and making disciples, pastoring, developing ministries, church planting, and missions to which I admit is limited. I acknowledge that I am no expert but merely one who is trying to be teachable to God as I stumble and fall and get up and crawl and get up again and again, trying to run this glorious race He has set before me.

WHY SIMPLE DISCIPLESHIP
To Hasten The Wedding

Table of Contents

A Portrait of Jesus
Choose the Better Thing

Suggested Reading

WHY SIMPLE DISCIPLESHIP
To Hasten The Wedding

1. *MY STORY*

My story is not an autobiography, as I did not write it. It was written by Another (Psalm 139:16). Fixing my eyes on my God and Saviour Jesus Christ (Hebrews 12:2), for *He* is the sovereign Author and faithful Finisher of my faith.

Born

Born in the Philippines, you are also automatically a Catholic, as many Filipinos assert. Basically, Filipino equals Catholic. Therefore, you must be raised Catholic. I think that is how it goes. Not too sure, really, because shortly afterward, I came to America when I was only five years old and grew up at the shore, the wet, wild, and crazy Jersey Shore.

Fifteen years later, in the mid-'80s, I revisited the Philippines. While hanging out with cousins and friends, there was this quiet guy who was there some of the time. Not in a creepy quiet way. He was friendly, just quiet. He hung around the peripheral, if you know what I mean. So, he did not really stick out to me but, God helped me to remember that he was there, or kind of there on the fringes. I also remember that he always seemed to have a Bible in his hands or his back pocket. Perhaps that is why I did not really notice him, because as a Catholic, I was not really interested in the Bible, having never read one. It just collected dust on our shelf. Sorry, correction: I have a Filipino mom, so our big Bible did not collect dust, but I do not recall it ever being opened or read, not by me anyway.

Born Again

Born and *born again* in the Philippines. There is a lot to my testimony and I do love sharing how God orchestrated it all, but that is not the purpose of this book. Long story short and as a popular Jewish comedian from the 90s would say, "*yada yada yada*," I became a Christian when my Tito (uncle) Jun helped me see from God's Word that because of my sin I deserved hell and God's wrath; that there was nothing in me or about me and nothing I could do to merit God's favor or forgiveness. So, he shared with me the Gospel of Jesus Christ. God opened my eyes to see my desperate need for Him and His forgiveness. He caused me to be born-again and I surrendered my life to Jesus as my God, my Lord and my Saviour. I became a Christian, a worshiper of Jesus! On my 30+ hours trip back to the States, I almost finished reading my first Bible that Tito Jun gifted me, which had belonged to my Lola (grandmother).

Before this, Catholicism was all I knew regarding religion, which was not very much. I knew even less about all the Christian churches, other than they were confusing with the many different denominations. My conclusion was that the Church could not figure itself out, and I wanted no part of the confusion. All I wanted was to know Jesus more, know His Word more, and follow Him as He called and commanded me (Mark 1:17).

So that is what I did. I worked, continued to read my Lola's Bible, and listened to the Bible teachings of John MacArthur and J. Vernon McGee on Family Radio 94.7FM. Those were the first Bible teachers God gave me—a solid biblically doctrinal foundation for a new baby Christian.

Do you remember the Puka shell necklaces back in the '70s? Well, that was my father's fault. He introduced those in the U.S. when he and my mom were needing a new income source. It was a huge success. When I joined our family business in New York City, one of my roles was corresponding and ordering from our Philippines office via telex, if any of you can remember that dinosaur communication network. We had to pay per character if I remember correctly, so we "*abbrv8d so tht we cud sav $*." This was long before pagers, cell phones, and texting, so I was already quite an expert when those finally came around years later.

At the end of my telex messages, I began to add "*The Word of the Day*" with a Bible passage or two. I knew it would cost, but I was excited about becoming a worshiper of Jesus and was eager to share the truth of His Word and salvation through Him alone. I did not know if anyone would pay much attention, but I sent the verses anyway.

A few months after I had started *"The Word of the Day,"* we needed more help at our N.Y. office. I sent a telex to the Philippines requesting them to send over one or two people. And they did send someone—that same guy who hung around me and my cousins, the friendly guy with the Bible! Everyone called him Boy, and he came to work at our office and to live in my house.

Because I was still a young, self-centered immature Christian who did not know much about serving others, Boy cooked and cleaned up the house. And you know, he never seemed to mind unless I was totally oblivious to it, which is very likely. At the office, Boy served clients, shipped packages, ran errands, took care of inventory, and cleaned up. He did a lot, again not seeming to mind at all.

Discipled

Here was Boy, serving me by cooking and cleaning and working for me in my father's company, with joy! I do not remember a moment of grumbling or complaining from him. I remember experiencing a slow period in our business, and Boy was working, while singing with joy!—and loudly exclaiming, *"Thank You, Jesus, for our trials!"* And I was like, *"What?! Thank You Jesus, for our trials*?!" And without  skipping a beat in his work, he quickly responded and resounded happily, *"Yup! Thank You, Lord, for our trials."* He then began to teach me how it is easy to trust God when times are trouble-free. But when times are not so easy is when God really grows our faith in Him.

And in my current battle against covid right now as I am writing this, he shared with me again just last night the same wise counsel and encouragement, *"It is in those times where we are*

in the valley that indeed our Shepherd picks us up into refuge."
Thank you, Boy.

In opening our home to people, he also taught me about hospitality. We would invite friends and anyone on Saturday nights, and Boy would lead us in a time of worship and prayer for missionaries and missions. Before I became a Christian, I had been a professional musician. Boy taught me how to use that gift of music to lead God's people to worship Him. These memorable weekly worship and prayer nights are where my passion for missions and the Unreached was birthed with the help of a guy introduced by Boy, my friend, Jim Cooper, with Operation Mobilisation at that time.

Boy also taught me to pray. Aside from Saturday worship and prayer nights, we also prayed together spontaneously throughout the week. I remember praying with Boy and seeing him literally cry out loud to God with tears for our family and for the lost. One particular night, we were praying in the family room. Boy was praying emotionally, but then he began to pray in a different language—*NOT* Filipino. Uhm... this kinda freaked me out but not nearly as much as when he prayed even louder in that "new language" and then grabbed my hand! I confess—I think I jumped! This began the wonderful lessons on the Holy Spirit for this young disciple.

These are vivid memories and foundational lessons for me. Every time I share this story about my time with Boy, I always say what a beautiful picture of Christ he was to me—serving me as our Lord Jesus *"came not to be served, but to serve,"* (Mark 10:45 ESV), and teaching me as Jesus taught those for whom He had compassion because they were like sheep without a shepherd (Mark 6:34). Is that not an awesome picture of Christ serving and teaching?

Boy would later tell me that though the company in the Philippines sent him to the States to work, there was more behind it. His Thursday evening prayer group, Acts 29, found out I had become a Christian. *They* were reading my *"Word of the Day"* verses and began to pray for me. As they prayed, they believed the Holy Spirit was leading them to send him here to the other side of the world. Why? He said, *"To disciple you."* I was not fully aware of it, but I was being discipled to become a disciple-maker of disciple-makers.

Now, you are probably wondering, *"Is Boy really his name? What a slam to call someone, "Boy," who works for you and cleans your house!"* Before you get your knickers all bunched up and out of sorts, as I understand it, Boy is a term of endearment in the Philippines, not used as a derogatory insult as it is in other countries. On the contrary, it is a name of affection, the name of my very first discipler, which I even use now for my first-born son, Runner, whom I also named after my first Bible teacher, MacArthur.

Would you like to know Boy's real name? This is yet another amazing part of this testimony as it almost completes the picture of Christ he was to me as he discipled me by serving me and teaching me. Boy's real name… Wait for it… is *"Emmanuel,"* which means *"God with us"* (Isaiah 7:14 ESV, Matthew 1:23 ESV). What?! Expository teaching and biblically sound foundation from MacArthur and McGee. And discipled by Emmanuel! Is my God good or what?! He is way too good to me.

I can go on and on about all the things that Boy taught me, showed me, and what I observed, as well. I will always be grateful for being able to follow him as he followed Jesus. This was an incredible and foundational gift from God at the very beginning of my new Christian life. It is what I have tried to emulate throughout the years since—opening my life and being available to others, telling them, *"Our house is open 25 hours a day,"* and sincerely meaning it! Feeding many with burgers, BBQ, and Bible. Worshiping and working together. Praying and playing together. Serving and celebrating together. Rejoicing and grieving together. Doing serious and silly stuff together. Rather simple really—just doing everyday normal life together as Boy did with me, and as Jesus did with His disciples.

Busyness

A little over a year later, Boy went back to the Philippines. I was already experiencing New-Testament-Church in our house, but I started visiting a traditional church anyway because that is what we are supposed to do, yes? Well, as soon as this church found out I was a singer and musician, they quickly recruited me for the music ministry. And since I was young and had way too much energy to burn, I was immediately signed up for youth ministry as well. So, I left the family business because I wanted to focus on full-time (not-yet-paid) ministry and missions.

Through the strong urging of my friend Jim, I joined Operation Mobilisation. Our small missionary team went to the small town of Val-d'Or, about 600 kilometres northwest of Montreal. Leading worship for the conference was exciting. Leading it in newly-learned broken French was, shall we say, *intéressant*, or interesting. Door-to-door evangelism, street witnessing, drama and music ministry, and writing and singing my testimony—in French! What was really exciting was meeting with many folks who did not know Jesus. I loved meeting people who never heard the Gospel! One, in particular, was a young guy named Gabriel from the neighboring town of Malartic.

Gabriel hung out with the team and I every day. He ate with us. Played with us. Went to every one of our outreaches. Heard all the songs and testimonies along with the Bible being preached. He watched as we prayed and worshiped. And he asked many questions which I tried my best to answer. Eventually, he confessed that this new Good News that he heard and saw in us was not something he could continue to deny. I believe Gabriel surrendered his life to Jesus.

It still breaks my heart today, leaving Gabriel without a discipler to help him grow and mature in his new life. It was then that I resolved to no longer do missions or ministry that way again—to not leave people without anyone to follow up and disciple them. Just Simple Discipleship, again as Boy did with me, and as Jesus did with His.

Well, back to full speed ahead of "normal life" in Jersey, church, and youth ministry, which consumed me and evolved into a full-time job at another church for a whopping $50 per week! Woohoo! But $50 did not go very far in 1990 in Jersey, so I had to work another full-time 40+ hours gig at Nordstrom's because I had bills to pay.

You know how people in Jersey say Nebraska? "*NeBRASka*!?!"

Well, yada yada yada... Fast-forward a few years later to join a new church in Nebraska where I was later ordained. I was busy, really busy leading the music team, Sunday morning music, Sunday night preaching and music, Wednesday night leadership (CREW and the S.L.A.V.E.s–Sound Light Audio Visual Engineers), College & Career Group (No Longer Children), co-leading men's ministry, and all the study and prep time for these. I was also responsible for the building and school maintenance. There were meetings, meetings, and would you believe, even more meetings. I became the administrator of our Christian school, teaching Bible and Chapel and studying and preparing for both, teaching Performing Arts, which included co-writing, directing, and performing two new musicals each year, and fundraising. A fun highlight of my week was spending Wednesday afternoons with the Forerunners: discipling the upperclassmen so that they might disciple the younger students.

I was also trying my best to balance that with my marriage and caring for and raising four young children at the time. And discipling a few guys, while also meeting with the men who were discipling me and the brothers who sharpened me. At this point, all these "necessary" ministry-traditions consumed my schedule. I thought, "*If we just get more volunteers and train more leaders, it will get easier.*" Wrong. As the church grew, so did the busyness and stress, even with more help and more leaders. Do not make the mistake of assuming that as things get bigger, they will get easier, far from it.

When anyone tells me how busy their life is, I just grin. Because I know busy. I am not bragging about doing all the above. Nor am I complaining or grumbling about it. It was just wrong. So wrong and way too much. Too much to the point where even though I felt guilty about it, one day I had to tell the other leaders, "*Something's gotta give! Or my marriage will. We are going to snap!*" After they grasped my desperation, I stood before the church and told them that I had to step down from leading Sunday morning music for a few months.

Now, of course, I still had to continue all the other ministry-traditions. They were, you know, "indispensable." But hey, stepping down from Sunday morning lightened the load a little bit so my family could breathe again.

Fast-forward again about 10 years to Colorado, and we began a church that met in our home and neighborhood clubhouse. My heart was always to reach out to unbelievers and unchurched people, intentionally trying *not* to tempt or draw people away from other churches, or "sheep-stealing." Now because I was focused on reaching unbelievers and the unchurched, guess who made up the majority of those who came to the clubhouse and our house? Unbelievers and unchurched people who tended to be young or not-yet-mature believers. Go figure, right?

We had at least 100 people in our house for one Thanksgiving celebration! But caring for young believers and pre-believers meant carrying all of Sunday preaching, marriage counseling, men's ministry, music ministry, sound ministry, Bible studies, youth ministry, park outreaches, homeless ministry, hospitality, set up, feeding, tear down, clean up, marketing, etc., *while* caring for my young family *and* starting a new business at the same time.

Burnout

Though I was extremely busy, I will admit I was still very excited and thrilled to be involved with all the ministry and pouring myself out into so many folks. So, I justified the busyness by convincing myself that all this busyness of church business was necessary and worth all my time and energy. Besides, this is the way everyone else is doing it and has always done it, so this must be the way. But all the excitement, justifying, and convincing I mustered up could not prevent the inevitable.

Young family. New business. New house-church. Yes, I was that arrogant to think I could do it all. I was spiraling down. That is until I believe I heard the Lord gently and firmly say, "*Stop.*"

From God's Word, I was able to know that He was not saying, "*Stop caring for your family*" or, "*Stop working.*" I also knew He was not saying, "*Stop being Church, preaching His Word, and making disciples.*" Those things are clear commands in God's Word, and He will not contradict His own Word.

- Loving and nourishing my wife (Ephesians 5:25-33)
- Caring for my children (Ephesians 6:4)
- Providing for my family (1 Timothy 3:4-5, 5:8)
- Gathering and being Church (Acts 2:42, Hebrews 10:25)
- Preaching the Word (2 Timothy 4:2)
- Making disciples (Matthew 28:18)

Therefore, through the process of elimination, God was telling me to stop all the unnecessary ministry-traditions, not because they were bad or wrong, but they were *"unauthorized fire which He did not command"* which I learned later. I was doing too much. I was doing more than necessary.

All this to say, I get it. I understand first-hand how church planting, ministry-traditions, and new ministry-traditions are exciting and pump up your adrenaline. To be totally transparent, I confess it can also feed your ego. It sure fed mine. And I ate it up for a while.

But I also know that it is tons of nonstop work, time-consuming, energy-draining, resource-depleting, properly hard, and just downright exhausting. Hence, why there is a need for Simple One-on-One Life-on-Life Discipleship—why we must go back to Discipleship According to Jesus, OG Discipleship, for you old-schoolers.

Earlier today on the phone, someone shared with me how they cried from being so exhausted from just recently starting a new church plant.

Unfortunately, we are not alone.

Practical Application Questions:

A. What is your story?

_____

_____

_____

_____

_____

2. Who are the people the Holy Spirit has placed in your life who influenced you, motivated you, taught you, guided you?

_____

_____

_____

_____

D. What have you learned or are learning from them?

_____

_____

_____

_____

Write a note to thank them personally.

Take some time right now, as much time as you need, to thank God for His wise and purposeful sovereignty.

Pick a verse from this chapter to memorize this week to hear God's voice.

Pray this verse back to God.

Sing to Him a song of reflective worship.

SONG FOR REFLECTIVE WORSHIP
Blessed Assurance by Fanny J. Crosby[5]

Blessed assurance, Jesus is mine!
Oh, what a foretaste of glory divine!
Heir of salvation, purchase of God,
Born of His Spirit, washed in His blood.

This is my story
This is my song
Praising my Saviour all the day long
This is my story
This is my song
Praising my Saviour all the day long

Perfect submission, perfect delight,
Visions of rapture now burst on my sight;
Angels descending, bring from above
Echoes of mercy, whispers of love.

This is my story
This is my song
Praising my Saviour all the day long
This is my story
This is my song
Praising my Saviour all the day long

Perfect submission, all is at rest,
I in my Saviour am happy and blest.
Watching and waiting, looking above,
Filled with His goodness, lost in His love.

This is my story
This is my song
Praising my Saviour all the day long
This is my story
This is my song
Praising my Saviour all the day long

PRAYER JOURNAL

_____

_____

_____

_____

_____

_____

_____

_____

_____

_____

_____

_____

_____

_____

_____

_____

_____

_____

_____

_____

2. A SHARED STORY

Sad to say, but mine is not an isolated story. *"It is not a non-unexclusive story"* (Nomel Phillips). Chew on that triple-negative awhile.

No. It is a story shared by too many. Speaking from my experiences and hearing and reading the personal stories from many others, traditional ministry and church planting are exciting. But they will also admit that it is nonstop, time-consuming, energy-draining, resource-depleting, and just downright exhaustingly hard work.

The following statistics of men who pastor and testimonies of volunteers should make us stop, question and rethink what we are doing.

Bad News of Burnout

Burnt
- 100% had a close associate or seminary buddy who had left the ministry because of burnout, conflict in their church, or from a moral failure.
- 89% considered leaving the ministry.
- 80% of seminary and Bible school graduates who enter the ministry will leave the ministry within the first five years.
- 71% stated they were burned out, and they battle depression beyond fatigue on a weekly and even a daily basis.
- 1,500 leave the ministry *each month* due to moral failure, spiritual burnout, or contention in their churches.
- 9 out of 10 will not retire in that role.

Disheartened
- 80% feel unqualified and discouraged in their role.
- 75% felt they were unqualified and/or poorly trained by their seminaries to lead and manage the church or to counsel others. This left them disheartened in their ability to pastor.
- 70% constantly fight depression.

- 50% are so discouraged that they would leave the ministry if they could but have no other way of making a living.

Overworked and Overwhelmed
- 90% work between 55 to 75 hours per week.
- 75% experience a significant crisis that they faced due to stress in the ministry.
- 54% find the role of pastoring overwhelming.

Undernourished and Unprepared
- 90% feel they were not adequately trained to cope with ministry coordination and the demands of the congregation.
- 72% said the only time they spend studying the Word is when they are preparing their sermons.
- 53% report that the seminary did not prepare them for the ministry.

Broke and Isolated
- 77% feel they do not have a good marriage.
- 70% say they're grossly underpaid.
- 70% do not have someone they consider to be a close friend.
- 63% of pastor's wives feel finances is a prime source of stress for their family.
- 57% unable to pay their bills.
- 57% said they would leave if they had a better place to go—including secular work.
- 50% do not meet regularly with an accountability person or group.
- 50% of marriages will end in divorce.

Unhealthy
- 90% stated they are frequently fatigued and worn out on a weekly and even daily basis (did not say burned out).
- 85% have never taken a Sabbatical
- 75% of ministers are extremely or highly stressed.

These are actual statistics from Bill Gaultiere[6] and from Dr. Richard J. Krejcir's ongoing research since 1989.[7]

Folks, read those numbers again. All 50% and above! These are far worse than any pandemic statistics! While burnout, discouragement, and relational breakdowns are not contagious, they are still being passed onto others. Every day! Too many people continue in this same busyness solely because *"this is the way it has always been done."* My brother-in-law, Jesse, an epidemiologist who has been tirelessly researching the covid virus all of 2020 to the present, said not regarding the pandemic, but the burnout statistics, *"It is devastating."*

Volunteers Not Spared

It is not only the professionals who get discouraged, over-scheduled, and burnt out. While most men who pastor have good intentions, they take on more than they should and continue to pass down the same traditional model to the people they hire and recruit. Many volunteers experience relational conflict and breakdown, discouragement, and spiritual problems. They too burn out and quit, sometimes for years or for good.

Here are a few sad testimonies:

"A Portrait of Burnout:
Let's see how Sunday School teacher, committee leader, choir member, new father Steve burned himself out. For starters, he didn't fully anticipate the challenge and difficulty of ministering to junior high kids. In fact, he had to push himself most Sunday mornings to go to class. He thought that singing in the choir would be fun but hadn't reckoned on all the rehearsal time, special performances (such as every night of the revival), and his need to practice at home.
Steve joined the building committee thinking he could help supervise the grounds maintenance crew. Instead, he wound up mowing the grass himself. And the building committee wasn't always one big happy family, especially when it came time to discuss the annual facilities budget.
Steve felt guilty whenever he missed a church function, like the Sunday night his new daughter was born, and the church

had its annual anniversary potluck supper. Eight people asked him where he'd been, and Steve couldn't determine if they truly cared about him or were checking up on him. Feeling that way made him feel even more guilty.

While Steve's wife, and junior high helper, recouped from the birth of their fourth child, Steve tried to find a temporary helper to fill in. Three people said working with junior high "wasn't their thing." Two wanted to "pray about it," and the one guy who promised to help out "for a little while" never showed up.

Steve's recent job promotion didn't help matters either, because now he's on the road more. But at least the modest pay increase would ease the financial expense of his new daughter.

When the youth minister finally corralled Steve about his "duty and responsibility" to attend every night of the revival, Steve didn't get mad, he just went limp and started thinking about the "small, simple" church his family used to belong to and how nice it would be to return.

Steve's trying experience is all too familiar to a growing number of conscientious Christians today who unknowingly fit the burnout syndrome to a "T" (Phil Van Auken).[8]

"For some time, I've felt burned-out, exhausted, stressed, and depressed. I talked to the elders of our church, but they suggested I just needed more public recognition for my efforts. (I don't!) And they made me feel guilty about even considering stepping down or taking a break. Now I feel if I do, the ministry-traditions will fail due to lack of leadership and everyone will blame me. What should I do?" (Mary Jane).[9]

"You could never quit. Doesn't matter how long you've been doing it. It didn't matter how exhausted you were. You were made to feel guilty to take a break or quit" (Robbi).

Thomas S. Rainer shared even more sad testimonials of burnout from volunteers that you can read on this website: <u>Five Common Reasons Church Members Burnout (churchanswers. com)</u>. Read the comments of the article.[10]

Throughout my limited involvement at different churches, house churches, church plants, church splits, church restorations, various ministry-traditions, and missions organizations, I know men and women who have quit doing ministry and left their church due to exhaustion, spiritual burnout, irreconcilable conflict with their churches, or moral failure. You may be feeling this right now or have felt this way. And you probably know many others.

The statistics and testimonies are cumulative and widespread. These things have been happening, are still happening, and will continue to happen.

Practical Application Questions:

1. What jumped out from the above statistics? Why is that significant to you? How do you relate to any of the sad testimonies of the volunteers?

_____

_____

_____

_____

_____

2. What do you think are the primary reasons people burn out? Are there places where you feel current church practices are making people do for Jesus more than be with Jesus?

_____

_____

_____

_____

_____

3. Jesus promises the Holy Spirit, *"I will ask the Father, and He will give you another Helper, a Comforter, to be with you forever, even the Spirit of Truth… He dwells with you and will be in you."* What does this reveal of God's character?

_____

_____

_____

_____

_____

4. How is God's promise of the Holy Spirit a strength and a comfort?

_____

_____

_____

_____

_____

But Why?

These statistics and testimonies cannot be ignored. We need to ask ourselves, *"Why is all of this happening?"*

Jesus said, "It is the Spirit Who gives life; the flesh is no help at all. The Words that I have spoken to you are spirit and life." (John 6:63 ESV)

Jesus said, "Take My yoke upon you, and learn from Me, for I Am gentle and lowly in My heart, and you will find rest for your souls. For My yoke is easy and My burden is light." (Matthew 11:29-30 ESV)

"By this we know that we love the children of God, when we love God and obey His commandments. For this is the love of God, that we keep His commandments. And His commandments are not burdensome." (1 John 5:2-3 ESV)

"Jesus said, "If you abide in My Word, you are truly My disciples, and you will know the truth, and the truth will set you free." (John 8:31-32 ESV)

Jesus promises the Holy Spirit Who gives life. Our flesh is no help at all. Jesus' Words are spirit and life. His yoke is easy. His burden is light. His commandments are not burdensome. His Word is truth. The truth will set us free.

Since we have the promised Holy Spirit Who gives us life and dwells with us and in us, and since Jesus' Words are spirit and life, and since His yoke is easy and His burden is light, and since His commandments are not burdensome, and since His Word is truth and will set us free, then why? Why do we see these statistics of discouragement and ministry burnout? Why do we see these statistics of spiritual problems and relational breakdowns? It does not make sense if what Jesus said is true. It does not add up. Jesus did not lie and is not lying. His Word is truth (John 17:17, Psalm 119:160).

I am not trying to imply that the Christian life is trouble-free or without trials, as the prosperity preachers falsely promise. *"They all seek their own interests, not those of Jesus Christ"* (Philippians 2:21 ESV). Jesus never assures a life of health, wealth, ease, comfort or even safety. Suffering is very real for Christians, particularly on the other side of the world. In fact, Scripture tells us to *"not be surprised at the fiery trial when it comes upon* [us] *to test* [us] *as though something strange is happening to* [us]" (1 Peter 4:12). While there are real struggles and legitimate difficulties here in the west, in truth much of our "suffering" is more the inevitable consequence of our own decisions and doings, regardless of the best of intentions.

Jesus says His yoke is easy; then it should be easy. He says His burden is light; then it should be light. He says His commandments are not burdensome; then they should not be burdensome.

He says the truth is freeing and liberating and should not burden us, suffocate us, or imprison us.

Unless *we* are doing more than what God commands. Unless *we* are complicating what should be simple. Unless *we* are making His commands burdensome.

Practical Application Questions:

1. You are packing for an emergency trip but have too many things you would like to bring. Frontier limits you to one tiny bag. Obviously, you start with only what is necessary. List those first items:

_____

_____

_____

_____

_____

2. Think about your typical weekly schedule. If you find little or no blocks of time for your family, for Jesus, for personal Bible study, for hospitality, for one-anothering, for making disciples, what needs to "come out of your bag" to make room for only what is necessary?

_____

_____

_____

_____

_____

3. Jesus said His yoke is easy, His burden is light, His commandments are not burdensome, His Word is truth, and the Truth will set us free. What does this reveal of God's character?

_____

_____

_____

_____

_____

The Busyness of Church

How much work is actually involved in Church? How easy is it to plant and build? To maintain and to sustain? To be honest, it is a lot of time-consuming work. It drains all your energy. It uses up all your resources. It is properly hard and just downright exhausting.

For example, here is a short list of ministry-traditions:

Sunday morning programs. Sunday evening programs. Wednesday evening programs. Setup-Teardown-Clean up-*Repeat*. Men's ministry. Women's ministry. Marriage ministry. Singles ministry. Single Moms' ministry. Single Dads' ministry. Divorce ministry. Counseling ministry. Children's ministry. Vacation Bible School. Youth ministry. College ministry. Senior ministry. Music ministry. Drama ministry. Coffee shop ministry. Bagel bar ministry. Hospitality ministry. Greeting ministry. Benevolence ministry. Child-care. Sunday Schools. New Members Foundations Classes. Community outreaches. Guest services. Guest follow-ups. Building cleaning. Building maintenance. Remodeling. Renovations. Upgrades. Raising funds. Distributing funds. Administrative functions. Meetings. Meetings. And more meetings! Paying the bills—mortgage or rent, utilities, supplies, upkeep and replacements, salaries, etc. Then there is all the "needed" advertising for the church.

Marketing. Merchandising. Branding. Photography. Website. Social media.

That is just the short list off the top of my head! But there is something missing from this list. Go ahead and read it and reread it again. What is missing?

ALL the prep and study time for all those ministry-traditions! They do not just happen. It takes time to plan, prepare, study and get everyone on the same page, and all with humble and happy attitudes. That is not easy unless you are doing it all yourself. But then there is the bad news of that option, which is... you are doing it all yourself.

There is another thing missing from this list. Can you guess? It is missing from this list because it is missing in most churches. Actually, I have been a part of only one church where this one thing was a significant part of that church's ethos. Many folks from around the world and other parts of the country came to this small-town church specifically for this one thing. Can you guess? We were known for it because it was not just preached from the pulpit but part of the daily life of the church. I was exhorted by my friend, Greg Priebe, that no one should get involved in ministry before this one thing.

I was young and restless and did not want to waste any time, but Greg said there will be plenty to do. For now, just be discipled. The busyness of Church and the doing of it will not go away. Do not worry so much about doing. Focus on being. Greg, thank you.

> *"We need to leave our lusting for ever-larger spheres of Christian service and concentrate on seeing God for ourselves and finding the deep answer for life in Him. Then, even if we are located in the most obscure corner of the globe, the world will make a road to our door to get that answer. Our service of help to our fellows then becomes incidental to our vision of God, and the direct consequence of it"* (Roy and Revel Hession).[11]

In the same way that Jesus said, *"You always have the poor with you"* (Mark 14:7 ESV), we will always have ministry-traditions to do. If you are a new worshiper of Jesus, Woohoo! and Hallelujah! *"There will be more joy in heaven over one sinner who repents"* (Luke 15:7 ESV) But be resolved to *not* allow yourself to get recruited for ministry too early. The busyness of Church and the doing of it will not go away. For now, just be discipled and learn to disciple.

Discipleship is what is missing from that list above. Many pulpits only mention disciple-making when they read the passage from Matthew 28. But other than that, there is little mention of it, thus just a little or none happening at all. We have all but replaced disciple-making with program after program and event after event leaving people exhausted, discouraged, and overwhelmed.

Not overwhelmed yet by that ministry list? Check out this even longer list from Disciple Christian: Types/List of Christian Ministries[12] This list has unnecessarily grown to be so much longer than what we actually read in Scripture.

As my wife, the beautiful Robbi Gail, was casually perusing through a shopping catalogue we just received in the mail for some reason, I asked her, *"See anything good?"* She flipped a page and simply responded, *"Nothing we need."*

Some time ago, I was walking through Walmart with one of my boys. We were talking about him, his friends and normal Dad-and-son stuff. I cannot remember exactly what we saw in the store, but we remarked on how there was so much stuff to buy. This prompted him to say, *"You don't need what you don't need."* Wow! From the lips of children… (Matthew 21:16).

"You don't need what you don't need."

None of the things on that long list of ministry-traditions are bad. They are good. Wonderful even. But are they really necessary? Necessary as in without them we die. Necessary as in, we "need" to order this Cordless Deep Tissue Massage Thingy from this catalogue! It is supposed to give us a professional neck, back, shoulders, thighs, knees, and more massage. We need to order it, or we will die! We have long days, and yes, it would be nice to give one another a professional massage. But do we really "need" it? Would we die without it? *"You don't need what you don't need!"* Throw away those catalogues and turn off the late-night infomercials!

Friends, we are to be equipped for the work of ministering, which is *"for building up the body of Christ."* (Ephesians 4:11-12 ESV). Because *"as each has received a gift,"* we are to *"use it to serve one another"* (1 Peter 4:10 ESV).

But since the first century, since Acts 2, God's Church, or Acts 2-Church, has turned away from God's original design for His Church, which was to simply love one another by doing life together, serving one another, building up each other in love, making disciples and reaching the nations. From the start, ministering in God's Church meant *every* believer used their spiritual gift to serve one another, not just those who preached.

> When you come together, <u>each one</u> has a hymn, a lesson, a revelation, a tongue, or an interpretation. Let all things be done for building up. (1 Corinthians 14:26 ESV)

Serving one another. Building up each other in love. Helping each other to grow and mature and be fruitful. This is Simple Discipleship, making disciples and teaching them to observe all that Christ commanded (Matthew 28:19-20).

But somehow, this began to change. God's Church today no longer looks like Acts 2-Church. Ministering in the Church today has grown from simply making disciples to the list above (which is still growing by the way) into *"performing some religious act within a specific building which was called 'the church'"* (Body Life by Ray Stedman).[13]

Are the *"religious acts"* on the above list about doing life together and serving one another? Are they about building up each other and one-anothering one another? We will dive into more about one-anothering one another in a later chapter. But these ministry-traditions are a lot of work, time-consuming, energy-draining, resource-depleting, and exhausting. It is no wonder why so many burn out, quit, or leave the Church.

I know this all too well. Being consumed with ministry-traditions made me more vulnerable to our enemy's temptations and tactics, where I then gave in to sin, which devastated my family. Sadly, we are still feeling the effects of that, but praise God Who specializes in resurrecting that which is dead! Praise Him for His restoration and healing. If you remember, would you please pray for us?

Friends, we should be shocked, saddened, and sobered with the above statistics, but not completely surprised. While the long list of ministry-traditions is not exhaustive, it is exhausting just reading it and remembering, let alone trying to recruit, coerce, or beg enough volunteers to come alongside and carry some of the load.

On the following page, I will have you read the "Busyness" part of "My Story" again. There will be no change in the story. But let us see how it makes you feel as you read it again… or try to. Think of the emotions that well up inside you.

which consumed me and evolved into a full-time job at another church f
whopping $50 per week Woohoo But $50 did not go very far in 1990 in Jersey
had to work another full-time 40+ hours gig at Nordstrom's because I had bills to
You know how people in Jersey say Nebraska? *NeBRASka!?!* Well yada yada
Fast-forward a few years later to join a new church in Nebraska where I was
ordained I was busy really busy leading the music team Sunday morning m
Sunday night preaching and music Wednesday night leadership (CREW and
S.L.A.V.E.s) College & Career Group (No Longer Children) co-leading m
ministry and all the study and prep time for these I was also responsible for
building and school maintenance There were meetings meetings and would
believe even more meetings I became the administrator of our Christian sc
teaching Bible and Chapel and studying and preparing for both teaching Perform
Arts which included co-writing directing and performing two new musicals each
and fund-raising A fun highlight of my week was spending Wednesday afternc
with the Forerunners discipling the upperclassmen so that they might disciple
younger students I was also trying my best to balance that with my marriage
caring for and raising four young children at the time And discipling a few g
while also meeting with the men who were discipling me and the brothers
sharpened me At this point all these "necessary" ministry-traditions consumed
schedule I thought "*If we just get more volunteers and train more leaders, it wil*
easier" Wrong.As the church grew so did the busyness and stress even with n
help and more leaders Do not make the mistake of assuming that as things get bi;
they will get easier far from it When anyone tells me how busy their life is I just
Because I know busy I am not bragging about doing all the above Nor a
complaining or grumbling about it. It was just wrong So wrong and way too n
Too much to the point where even though I felt guilty about it one day I had to
the other leaders *Something's gotta give Or my marriage will We are going to s*
After they grasped my desperation I stood before the church and told them that I
to step down from leading Sunday morning music for a few months Now of cou
still had to continue all the other ministry-traditions They were you k
"indispensable" But hey, stepping down from Sunday morning lightened the lo;
little bit so my family could breathe again Fast-forward again about 10 year
Colorado and we began a church that met in our home and neighborhood clubhc
My heart was always to reach out to unbelievers and unchurched people, intention
trying *not* to tempt or draw people away from other churches or "sheep-steali
Now because I was focused on reaching unbelievers and the unchurched guess
made up the majority of those who came to the clubhouse and our house Unbelie
and unchurched people who tended to be young or not-yet-mature believers Go fi;
right We had at least 100 people in our house for one Thanksgiving celebration!
caring for young believers and pre-believers meant carrying all of Sunday preach

How far would you have gotten in this book or any book if the first page looked like the previous page? How far did you get on that one page? Did you even begin to read it, or was it too much? It is a very full page. Too full, yes?

It is a small example of how our lives look when they are packed to the extreme limits without any margin left. How did it make you feel? Claustrophobic? Suffocating? Confined? Smothered? Like being buried alive in a box? Imagine all the pages of this book like this. Imagine all the pages of every book like this. Does this resemble your life? Does this resemble the life of anyone you know?

We need margins on the pages. We need margins in our lives. If you also noticed, there were no commas or periods. Not only do we need margins, we also need commas to tell us to pause, break, relaaaaaxx. We need periods to help us see that something has come to an end, and we do not just run on to the next thing.

"What is worse than your being personally burned out, is that you're distracting your disciples from what should be their sole attention on Jesus. The busyness of church fills them up with activities and to-dos... Remember, we aren't trying to "strive to be a great man of God, but rather a man in whom GOD is great!" All these tasks and busywork may be making great men of God, but they are in fact distracting them from being men in whom God is great. What if these same men brought God with them to work, rather than always bringing their good works to God?" (Ezra Roizen).

Why are we so preoccupied with the business of the busyness of Church and ministry-traditions that are so time-consuming and devours most of our energy? Why, when it mostly results in discouragement, exhaustion, and burnout? It almost makes us wonder what sane, healthy person would do this on purpose.

Robbi said that when she used to work in a salon and a gal was pregnant and more gals were getting pregnant, they would begin to joke amongst themselves saying, *"It's in the water."* Perhaps we need to start asking, *"Is it in the water?"* Not jokingly, but seriously ask.

Practical Application Questions:

1. How are the ministry-traditions in your church keeping people too busy?

_____

_____

_____

_____

_____

2. How would you describe the busyness of Church? When have you felt too busy and over committed?

_____

_____

_____

_____

_____

3. Ministry-traditions are good, even helpful like a Cordless Deep Tissue Massage Thingy, but how are they really needed? Are they commanded in God's Word? If so, where? *"And the Lord said, 'let there be potluck!'"* (Ezra and Bambi Roizen).

_____

_____

_____

_____

_____

4. How is the Holy Spirit leading you to add "commas and periods"? To make some margin?

_____

_____

_____

_____

_____

Pick a verse or two from this chapter to memorize this week to hear God's voice.

Pray these verses back to God.

Sing to Him a song of reflective worship.

SONG FOR REFLECTIVE WORSHIP
And Can It Be That I Should Gain by Charles Wesley[14]

And can it be that I should gain
An interest in the Savior's blood?
Died He for me, who caused His pain
For me, who Him to death pursued?
Amazing love! How can it be
That Thou, my God, shouldst die for me?
Amazing love! How can it be
That Thou, my God, shouldst die for me?

'Tis mystery all: th'Immortal dies
Who can explore His strange design?
In vain the firstborn seraph tries
To sound the depths of love divine
'Tis mercy all! Let earth adore
Let angel minds inquire no more
'Tis mercy all! Let earth adore
Let angel minds inquire no more

He left His Father's throne above
So free, so infinite His grace
Emptied Himself of all but love
And bled for Adam's helpless race
'Tis mercy all, immense and free
For O my God, it found out me!
'Tis mercy all, immense and free
For O my God, it found out me!

Long my imprisoned spirit lay
Fast bound in sin and nature's night
Thine eye diffused a quickening ray
I woke, the dungeon flamed with light
My chains fell off, my heart was free
I rose, went forth, and followed Thee
My chains fell off, my heart was free
I rose, went forth, and followed Thee

Still the small inward voice I hear
That whispers all my sins forgiven
Still the atoning blood is near
That quenched the wrath of hostile Heaven
I feel the life His wounds impart
I feel the Savior in my heart
I feel the life His wounds impart
I feel the Savior in my heart

No condemnation now I dread
Jesus, and all in Him, is mine
Alive in Him, my living Head
And clothed in righteousness divine
Bold, I approach th'eternal throne
And claim the crown, through Christ my own
Bold, I approach th'eternal throne
And claim the crown, through Christ my own

Amazing love! How can it be
That Thou, my God, shouldst die for me?

PRAYER JOURNAL

3. IT'S IN THE WATER

The saying, *"It's in the water,"* is sarcastically used to say that there must be something in the water that is causing people to act or feel a certain way or maybe develop superpowers. In most cases, it is used to explain something negative, blaming the "water" for people's bad behavior or their poor health, not wanting to catch something perceived as possibly contagious. *"It must have been something they drank. It's in the water. So, don't drink the water."*

We enjoy watching adventure reality shows about surviving in the wild. In these shows, people are left as a group or alone on remote uninhabited islands. It is imperative that they find a good source of freshwater quickly.

In one episode of a show, after going two days without drinkable water, the people finally found fresh water, but it was stagnant, filthy, and highly questionable. They filtered it and boiled it. Although they were so positive and sincerely believed it would be safe to drink, they still got very sick.

In the last chapter, we saw the sad statistics due to the busyness of the Church. We saw how the results from this are mostly exhaustion, discouragement, and burnout, yet we continue to pursue this same traditional model over and over again. It should make us wonder why a sane, healthy person would do this purposely.

Perhaps it *is* in the water.

What is Evil?

What do people say is evil? Our good friend David Carducci took us out to Ruth's Chris Steakhouse, and I was chastised for asking our server for some ketchup, as if I did something evil. I can understand if I was putting pineapple on your pizza. That is like, the worst!

What is evil? Seriously, what would people say is evil? There are some people who even deny evil exists. If our eyes are truly open and we take a good hard look all around us and around the world, what would we see? Would we not see evil? What is evil? What would you say is evil?

Being called the b___ word, if you are a woman? Is that evil? What is evil? Corrupt, lying, self-serving career politicians? Homosexuality? Our country sadly celebrates National Coming Out Day—the widespread cultural celebration of the sin of homosexuality! How about Rape? Adultery? Divorce? Murder? What is the worst evil? Abortion? My friend Nathaniel was passionately sharing how every day abortion kills the same number of kids as in a typical high school as he was crying out to God for it to end. And there are millions of people who not only celebrate but demand and fight for this evil! Innocent, defenseless babies are willfully aborted, purposely harvested for who knows what. Evil! And if babies are not aborted, children are exploited, trafficked, and enslaved. Cebu is one of the most beautiful places you will see. Yet, it is also number one in the world for online sexual exploitation of children. When our friend, Glenn Edwards, was still with International Justice Mission in the Philippines, he and his team were able to rescue many young children, one even as young as only three months! Evil!

Almost every day on tv or online we and our families are incessantly being catechized in the world's inviolable evils of sexual perversions and confusions portrayed as truth and even as wholesome family values. Evil has become good and good has become evil. So sad.

What *is* the Worst?

We tend to overuse words or use them wrongly. *Love* for example. *"I love my wife and children. I love the Broncos! I love French Fries with brown gravy!"* Really?! Do we really *love* all those things? Or, how about the word *hate*? *"I hate sin! I hate this weather. I hate these shoes!"* We *hate* shoes like we *hate* sin? Or as we saw in the last chapter, the word *need*. *"I need air. I need a master bedroom with a private bathroom. I need that Cordless Deep Tissue Massage Thingamajig!"* What?! Inconceivable! I do not think those words mean what you think they mean (name that movie).

We also overuse phrases, like *"That's the worst."* What is the worst? Is it being called a b____? *"That's the worst."* Is it slow or no Wi-Fi? *"Oh, that's the worst."* Really? *That's* the worst?! Not homosexuality, rape, adultery, divorce, abortion, or the sexual exploitation of children? What *is* the worst? Obviously, there is Satan, and he is evil. What about in the Church? Slander? Gossip? Division?

Robbi was so distraught last night. It breaks her heart to hear of division in the Church and people choosing not to fellowship with other people. As we talked about it more, we concluded that it was more relational than doctrinal. My friend, David Bendinelli, would jokingly say, *"You know Jesus said where two or three are gathered... there will be conflict."* It is funny, yet true. When you have lived long enough, you know that offense and conflict are inevitable. Division is actually primarily due to unforgiveness and bitterness. One of the main problems in most churches is *not* doctrinal disagreement but relational breakdown. It is unforgiveness! Is this not evil in God's Church?

> *"Despite what many in the Church say, doctrine is not at the root of most divisions. The main problem is the shallowness or non-existence of our love for each other, which comes from a shallowness in our understanding of the Gospel. We have to grasp just how much God hates the division between His children—and our lackadaisical indifference to it"* (Francis Chan).[15]

Exodus 20:7 commands us to *"not take the Name of the Lord your God in vain"* My friend, Jerry Gross, considers this to be the "worst" sin, as it continues, *"for the Lord will not hold him guiltless who takes His name in vain"* (ESV). Jerry says, *"While many view this verse as referring to not cursing the Name of the Lord, the original Hebrew word, "nasah" means, "to carry; be lifted up, be exalted" rather than "take." The correct translation would actually mean, "You shall not carry, exalt, or uplift the Name of the Lord your God in vain." Thus, it more accurately refers to praising the Lord in vain, meaning do not justify evil in God's Name or misrepresent Who He is."* Just as Jesus said, *"in vain do they worship Me"* (Mark 7:7 ESV). Evil!

God's Word on Evil

More important than what people say or what you might think is evil, what does God's Word say is evil?

Acts 17:16 tells us Paul's *"spirit was provoked within him"* (ESV). What could have provoked a man who wrote, *"Love is patient and kind; love does not envy or boast; it is not arrogant or rude. It does not insist on its own way; it is not irritable or resentful; it does not rejoice at wrongdoing but rejoices with the truth. Love bears all things, believes all things, hopes all things, endures all things. Love never ends"* (1 Corinthians 13:4-8 ESV)? And in Ephesians 4:32, *"Be kind to one another, tenderhearted..."* (ESV). Can you imagine someone who wrote these things being provoked? The word provoked in Greek is παρωξύνετο (pronounced pah-roh-Xu-neto) which means being roused to burn with anger. Paul, who wrote love is not irritable, but tenderhearted; his spirit was roused to burn with anger! What on earth could have provoked Paul?

Idols. *"He saw that the city was full of idols."* Why was he provoked by other people having idols? Because idols take the place of God.

At one church, a person went up to the front and began to share, *"I see Jesus on the cross looking out at all of you and saying, 'YOU* (pointing to the congregation) *are worthy of it all."* Blasphemy! Jesus is worthy of it all, not us! The cross is about the glory of God, not the glory of man. **The glory of GOD!** It is not about how valuable we are or how we are worth the price of His blood, because the truth is we are not. What that person shared that morning attempted to take the glory that belongs only to God and place it on people! That was not the Gospel but a totally different gospel. Had Paul been there, he would have said his spirit was provoked within him.

What does God say is evil? *"Be appalled, O heavens, at this; be shocked, be utterly desolate,"* declares the Lord, *for My people have committed two evils: they have forsaken Me, the Fountain of living waters, and hewed out cisterns for themselves, broken cisterns that can hold no water"* (Jeremiah 2:12-13 ESV).

We could list many evils in this world and even in His Church because there are many. In this passage in Jeremiah, God is not only telling us what is evil, but what makes evil, evil, the evilest evil, the evil that provoked Paul, the evil that should also provoke us, appall us, shock us, and utterly ruin us.

Here is more of God's Word on evil:

"You have done more evil than all who lived before you. You have made for yourself other gods... you have aroused My anger and turned your back on Me" (1 Kings 14:9 ESV).

"Samuel replied. 'You have done all this evil; yet do not turn away from the LORD'" (1 Samuel 12:20 ESV).

"For rebellion is like the sin of divination, and arrogance like the evil of idolatry. Because you have rejected the Word of the LORD" (1 Samuel 15:23 ESV).

"Our parents were unfaithful; they did evil in the eyes of the LORD our God and forsook Him. They turned their faces away from the LORD's dwelling place and turned their backs on Him" (2 Chronicles 29:6 ESV).

"Then the Israelites did evil in the eyes of the LORD and served the Baals. They forsook the LORD, the God of their ancestors, Who had brought them out of Egypt. They followed and worshiped various gods of the peoples around them. They aroused the LORD's anger because they forsook Him and served Baal and the Ashtoreths... the people returned to ways even more corrupt than those of their ancestors, following other gods and serving and worshiping them. They refused to give up their evil practices and stubborn ways" (Judges 2:11-13, 19 ESV).

"Does the snow of Lebanon ever vanish from its rocky slopes? Do its cool waters from distant sources ever stop flowing? Yet My people have forgotten Me; they burn incense to worthless idols, which made them stumble in their ways..." (Jeremiah 18:14-15 ESV).

"You shall have no other gods before Me. You shall not make for yourself a carved image, or any likeness of anything that is in heaven above, or that is in the earth beneath, or that is in the water under the earth. You shall not bow down to them or serve them, for I the Lord your God Am a jealous God," (Exodus 20:3-4 ESV).

"You have praised the gods of silver and gold, of bronze, iron, wood, and stone, which do not see or hear or know, but the God in Whose hand is your breath, and Whose are all your ways, you have not honoured" (Daniel 5:23 ESV).

"I Am the Lord; that is My Name; My glory I give to no other, nor My praise" (Isaiah 42:8 ESV).

"And He [Jesus] said to them, 'Well did Isaiah prophesy of you hypocrites, as it is written, "This people honours Me with their lips, but their heart is far from Me. In vain do they worship Me, teaching as doctrines the commandments of men.' You leave the commandment of God and hold to the tradition of men"' (Mark 7:6-7 ESV).

"For the wrath of God is revealed from heaven against all ungodliness and unrighteousness of men, who by their unrighteousness suppress the truth. For what can be known about God is plain to them, because God has shown it to them. For His invisible attributes, namely, His eternal power and divine nature, have been clearly perceived, ever since the creation of the world, in the things that have been made. So, they are without excuse. For although they knew God, they did not honour Him as God or give thanks to Him, but they became futile in their thinking and their foolish hearts were darkened. Claiming to be wise, they became fools, and exchanged the glory of the immortal God for images resembling mortal man and birds and animals and reptiles. Therefore, God gave them up in the lusts of their hearts to impurity, to the dishonouring of their bodies among themselves because they exchanged the truth about God for a lie and worshipped and served

the creature rather than the Creator, Who is blessed forever!
Amen" (Romans 1:18-25 ESV).

"Love does not delight in evil but rejoices with the truth" (1 Corinthians 13:6 ESV).

What makes evil the most evil, God says, is not all those horrible things we mentioned earlier. The evilest evil is forsaking Him, deserting Him, rejecting Him, turning away from Him, forgetting Him, being indifferent toward Him. All those other things are horrific and terrible, yes, evil, yes, but they are only the evil fruit of the evilest evil of forsaking God and preferring our own way.

Now, notice God does not say, *"My people are evil because they are not thirsty."* He does not say that because we are.

We Are Thirsty Beings

God says His people have committed two evils. The first is forsaking Him. The second is making broken cisterns for ourselves. Why do people make cisterns? Primarily for drinking. So, it is not that they lack thirst or are not thirsty. They *are* thirsty. You are thirsty. We are thirsty beings. We worship. We meditate. We are thirsty. We are worshipping, meditating, thirsty beings.

- Whom are you worshiping?
- On what do you meditate most of your day?
- Where are you quenching your thirst?

We *"are a people who go astray"* in our heart (Psalm 95:10 ESV), *"like sheep"* (1 Peter 2:25 ESV). See also Isaiah 53.

"Prone to wander, Lord, I feel it; prone to leave the God I love…"[16]

We go astray. Prone to wander. Prone to leave. We wander because our attention is distracted, and our affections are diverted. What is distracting our attention? What is diverting our affections? Where are we drinking?

41

According to the latest 2020 data from Broadbandsearch.net,[17] the average time a person spends on social networking is up to 144 minutes per day. 144 minutes! Over two hours on social media. How can this be healthy?

Jim Cooper used to call the tv a *"brain-sucker."* Do we even want to know how much time is being wasted in front of the television? It is even more than the time squandered on social media—hours more! We binge hours upon hours on social media and tv without even cracking open our Bibles for a little sip!

"Prone to wander, Lord, I feel it; prone to leave the God I love…"[18]

Friends, our bodies need water, or else we die. Even more so, our souls, who we really are, need living water, or else we die. The people are not evil because they are not thirsty. They are evil because they *are* thirsty, but not thirsty for God!

Broken Cisterns

So, the reality is that we are thirsty. That means we are drinking. But drinking what? Drinking from where? Here is the word picture:

Picture The Fountain in the middle of an endless desert, refreshing, cool, sparkling, life-giving water overflowing and pouring with all Its goodness, freely inviting and offering you to drink to your heart's content. But instead, you look at It with indifference and turn away from It. You not only turn your back to It but, because you are thirsty, you turn to a mirage that deceives you into thinking it will quench your thirst. So, believing the lie, you turn away from The Fountain for the mirage and begin to dig in the sand. You start digging in the crusty dusty ground, working and sweating to make these things that do not even work. They are broken and dirty, and yet you try to somehow quench your thirst from it. Why? Because you are thirsty! And all the while, God, The Fountain of living waters, is freely offering you as much living water as you can drink! Thus, 1) Forsaking God, The Fountain of living waters, and 2) quenching your thirst, or unsuccessfully trying to, from broken cisterns that can hold no water. *"Two great evils!*" our God says. If that does not affect you, melt you, or move you in any way, then something is wrong!

Remember the garden where our first parents first sinned? What was their first sin? Was it the eating of the fruit? *"So, when the woman saw that the tree was good for food, and that it was a delight to the eyes, and that the tree was to be desired to make one wise, she took of its fruit and ate, and she also gave some to her husband who was with her, and he ate."* (Genesis 3:6 ESV). It all started in their hearts and minds *before* they ate. They forsook God and His Word and satiated themselves in the tree of the knowledge of good and evil. The sin of self-divinity! And we are not told what fruit they ate. Do you know why? We have such a doing-mentality and a legalistic bent that will simply say: *"Cannot eat apples. Apples bad. Apples evil."*

The cisterns were just broken, neither good nor bad. Back to Jeremiah, God does not say the cisterns are evil. He just says they are broken. He does not say they are good or bad. That would be too obvious. We know pornography is a broken cistern. We know drunkenness, adultery, and sex outside of marriage are broken cisterns.

But what about a godly marriage? A godly family? A successful career? A good reputation? If you are quenching your thirst there, that is idolatry because you have made your marriage, your family, your career, your reputation into cisterns, and they are not perfect. They are broken cisterns. Do not get me wrong. I love marriage. Marriage and sex are good. Really good! But marriage and sex are broken cisterns. Is family perfect? It is also a broken cistern. Are children perfect? If yours are like mine, they are perfect little angels, yes? Is education perfect? At the prices we pay, they better be perfect! Are careers perfect? And how about ministry? Hmm, well, the sad statistics from chapter two sure tell us otherwise how "perfect" they are.

These things are not evil. Not even bad. But broken cisterns, all. It **IS** in the water! Everything apart from God is a broken cistern that cannot hold living water.

"Whoever loves father or mother more than Me is not worthy of Me, and whoever loves son or daughter more than Me is not worthy of Me" (Matthew 10:37 ESV).

Drinking from broken cisterns is exactly like that cast of adventurers who wholeheartedly, sincerely, and so strongly believed they would be fine drinking the water they boiled from that stagnant putrid water source. Yet, they became terribly ill and would have gotten much worse if they did not stop

Forsaking God. Turning our backs on Him. Ignoring Him. And making broken cisterns to quench our thirsty souls. This is what makes evil, evil. This is the evilest evil. This is the worst.

Practical Application Questions:

1. Before reading this chapter, how did you describe evil? How did you describe the worst evil?

_____

_____

_____

_____

_____

2. What other "broken cisterns" can you name and describe where people are drinking?

_____

_____

_____

_____

3. Why is it so easy to drink from there? What makes them so inviting and appealing to drink there instead of at the Fountain of living water?

_____

_____

_____

_____

_____

4. What would your close friends and family say is the fountain of your strength, wisdom, and life?

_____

_____

_____

_____

_____

5. *"Whoever drinks of the water that I will give him will never be thirsty again. The water that I will give him will become in him a spring of water welling up to eternal life"* (John 4:14 ESV) What does this show you about God's character?

_____

_____

_____

_____

_____

Come and Drink

Can we repent of this? Is there any hope? Of course! After this terrible indictment, a few verses later, God says, *"Return. Return to Me O faithless ones. Return to Me"* (Jeremiah 3:11-22). This is good news, friends! This is amazingly good news. God, the Creator of the universe, the Fountain of living waters Whom we forsook and Whom we rejected is calling us, inviting us to turn from our evil ways and return to Him, to come and drink!

In John 4, our God and Savior Jesus Christ gives us this same invitation, *"You are here at the well obviously because you are thirsty. If you only knew the gift God is offering you right now, the gift of living water. Once you drink of It, this living water is always there to satisfy you, fill you, comfort you, nourish you, wash you, and quench the never-ending thirst of your soul. And this living water will become in you a spring, a well, a fountain, and you will never thirst again. Not because one drink is enough, but because drinking from This Fountain produces an eternal fountain in you for an eternity of drinks. This living water, which flows through and from Me, will give you life, abundant and eternal life, My Life!"*

You are thirsty, but thirsty for what? You are drinking, but drinking what? Acknowledge that you have not been or are now not thirsty for God. God calls our evil against Himself as the worst evil, the most evil, evil. Realize that forsaking God, quenching your thirst in other broken cisterns, is far worse than the worst evil that:

- Man has committed against himself–drunkenness, drug addiction, immorality,
- Man against fellow man–adultery, divorce, rape, murder, and
- Man against humanity–abortion, sexual exploitation, trafficking, slavery, genocide, socialism, and communism.

Do you want to know why you are not thirsty for God? It is not because you have drunk your fill of Him. It is because you have been drinking from other cisterns, broken cisterns. It *is* in the water! Repent. Stop drinking from broken cisterns. Turn away as they can hold no water. Hear His call and invitation to return. Come to The Fountain. Hear Jesus offer a drink of living water.

We need to stop focusing so much on doing and focus more on being. Being thirsty. Because we are thirsty. And if you are thirsty, you need a drink. So, drink. But drink from The Fountain.

The Wheel: Hub–Spokes–Rim

Many years ago, Dawson Troutman came out with a simple tool one can draw on a napkin to easily illustrate how each part — the Wheel — with the hub, the spokes, and the rim representing the life essentials for genuine Christian growth:

- For new Christians and new disciples: to think deeply and practically about how to begin his or her new God-centered, Christ-exalting, Spirit-filled, Bible-saturated, Prayer-fueled, Disciple-making, Missions-minded life.
- For already Christians, disciples, and not yet disciples: to think deeply and practically about living a God-centered, Christ-exalting, Spirit-filled, Bible-saturated, Prayer-fueled, Disciple-making, Missions-minded life.

The Hub is God at the center of your life. As The Center, The Fountain, we need to be spending regular, intimate time with Jesus every day, drinking from The Fountain. How is your Jesus Time?

I was speaking with my favorite son-in-law, Micah about this. Friends, it should not impress any of you to know that I eat at least two meals a day and that I drink at least 2-3 liters of water every day. Even in my most stressful and busiest week, somehow, I seem to find the time to grab a bite and drink. Are you impressed? No, because it is normal to eat and drink.

So, why are you so impressed when a brother or a sister in Christ is feasting at the table of the Lord every day? You are almost surprised to hear that they wake early to spend hours reading their Bibles and praying. Why? They are just feeding their hungry and thirsty souls.

What about *your* soul? Are you feeding your soul every day? Are you drinking from The Fountain? The heart of the man or woman of God is ever athirst for God.

The Vertical Spokes on the wheel: God's Word and Prayer. Do you have a daily healthy diet of God's Word? How is your prayer life? How is your personal study of God's Word? Are you drinking from there?

There is a Bible reading plan that helps you power-read the entire Bible in just 60 days. It sounds more difficult than it is. With this plan, you can read through the whole Bible in 60 days with just 30-40 minutes of daily reading. 30-40 minutes! That is really not a lot of time compared to 144 minutes people spend on social media every day. And this does not even count the time spent watching shows—eight hours every day and binge-watching three every week!

The Horizontal Spokes on the wheel flowing from the hub: Simple Discipleship and Fellowship.

<u>Simple Discipleship</u>: Our Lord calls us to be making disciples. How? First, by being discipled. But how? Find someone you respect and admire and simply ask. Learn from him or her. You want to grow in your Jesus Time and your love for Jesus? Be discipled by someone like Robbi, who loves Jesus so much more than she loves me. Ask someone like my friend, David Lewin, who chooses the better thing: sitting at Jesus' feet. You want to grow in your love for God's Word? Ask someone like Dick Snyder, who pastors in the Philippines and is always quick to initiate God's Word into almost every conversation. You want to grow in your prayer life? Ask people like prayer-warriors, Shelley Davy, and Micah, who lose themselves in the presence of God while praying. Or ask someone like Robbi who is so quick to pray at the drop of a hat whether in private or public.

<u>Fellowship</u>: This is where we grow together, live life together, one-another one another, engage in biblical fellowship and accountability, and become equipped to grow, mature, and be fruitful—Simple Acts 2-Church. (Next book? Hmmm...) A little more on this later in the book.

Acknowledge your thirst. You *are* thirsty. Drink from The Fountain. Jesus time. God's Word. Prayer. Discipleship and Fellowship. Start there. Start drinking there and quenching your thirst there. We all need to start there, being thirsty before doing, *before* serving, *before* ministry, which is the rim of the wheel where we as obedient Christians in action live out the Great Commandment, fulfilling the Great Commission, all to hasten the Great Consummation, the Wedding—the Joy of all joys!

Are sound systems and words on a screen good? They are helpful. Are they necessary for our walk and growth in the Lord? No. Drinking from The Fountain is. Are youth group or children's ministry-tradition good things? Wonderful things! Are they necessary for our walk and growth in the Lord? No. Drinking from The Fountain is. Are playing piano or singing on stage good things? Sure! Are they necessary? No. Drinking from The Fountain is.

"You don't need what you don't need!"

What is necessary for your spiritual health and our spiritual health as His Church? Drinking. Drinking at The Fountain. Jesus Time. Being discipled. Acts 2-Church. Why? Because you *are* thirsty. And because you are thirsty, you *need* to drink. Why? Because our souls cannot live without living water.

How do we glorify The Fountain? Should we come with our cups and buckets full of our good works and pour them into the Fountain? In Psalm 116, does the psalmist say, "*What shall I render to the LORD for all His benefits to me? Should I pay Him back? Should I come with all my service? Should I add more of my water to His Fountain?*" No! We glorify The Fountain by coming thirsty, coming needy for a drink, and taking a deep mouthful and saying, "*Ahhh. Soo good! So good!*" The psalmist cries aloud, "*I will lift up my cup for more of YOU God! I want more. I want more. I want more!*"

"*With You is The Fountain of life*" (Psalm 36:9 ESV).

"Jesus said, '*Everyone who drinks of this water will be thirsty again* [for that water], *but whoever drinks of the water that I will give him will never be thirsty forever* [for that water]. *The water that I will give him will become in him a spring of water welling up to eternal life*'" (John 4:13-14 ESV).

"*If anyone thirsts, let him come to Me and drink*" (John 7:37 ESV).

"*As a deer pants for flowing streams, so pants my soul for You, O God. My soul thirsts for God, for the living God. When shall I come and appear before God?*" (Psalm 42:1-4 ESV).

"*O God, You are my God; earnestly I seek You; my soul thirsts for You; my flesh faints for You, as in a dry and weary land where there is no water. So, I have looked upon You in the sanctuary, beholding Your power and glory. Because Your steadfast love is better than life, my lips will praise You. So, I will bless You as long as I live; in Your Name, I will lift up my hands. My soul will be satisfied as with fat and rich food, and my mouth will praise You with joyful lips*" (Psalm 63:1-5 ESV).

Pause right now. Come to The Fountain and let your soul drink.
Pick a verse or three to memorize to hear God's voice.
Pray these verses back to God.
Sing to Him a song of reflective worship.

SONG FOR REFLECTIVE WORSHIP
There is a Fountain Filled With Blood by William Cowper[19]

There is a fountain filled with blood
Drawn from Immanuel's veins
And sinners plunged beneath that flood
Lose all their guilty stains
Lose all their guilty stains
Lost all their guilty stains
And sinners plunged beneath that flood
Lose all their guilty stains

The dying thief rejoiced to see
That fountain in his day
And there have I, though vile as he
Washed all my sins away
Washed all my sins away
Washed all my sins away
And there have I, though vile as he
Washed all my sins away

Dear dying Lamb, Thy precious blood
Shall never lose its pow'r
Till all the ransomed Church of God
Are safe to sin to more
Are safe to sin no more
Are safe to sin no more
Till all the ransomed Church of God
Are safe to sin no more

E'er since by faith I saw the stream
Thy flowing wounds supply
Redeeming love has been my theme
And shall be till I die
And shall be till I die
And shall be till I die
Redeeming love has been my theme
And shall be till I die

When this poor, lisping, stamm'ring tongue
Lies silent in the grave
Then in a nobler, sweeter song
I'll sing Thy pow'r to save
I'll sing Thy pow'r to save
I'll sing Thy pow'r to save
Then in a nobler, sweeter tongue
I'll sing Thy pow'r to save

PRAYER JOURNAL

4. ALL AND ONLY

Almost 30 years ago, my friend, Steve Busskohl, and I started a bible study for businessmen: Business Owners Scripture Study or B.O.S.S. With about 6-10 other fellas, we met on Wednesdays at the Arrow Stage Lines conference room.

I remember after one study, Steve and I were reviewing and assessing how it was going, how the men were doing, and our goal to not allow this to grow beyond what we were able, and more than our schedules could handle.

He and I both had wives and we were dads. He was an elder at our church and the owner of the bus company and a travel agency. I led worship and the music team and the College & Career Team, while working as a full-time car salesman at Cornhusker Auto Center. We were also being discipled and discipling other men throughout the week. We had full schedules and did not wish them to get any fuller.

Sitting at his conference table, Steve shared a principle with me that I have since shared many times over the years. The *"All and Only"* principle: *"Do ALL God commands. Do ONLY what God commands. Do all, not less. Do only, not more."* Because we are not yet perfect, because sin still dwells in our flesh (especially mine), because we still have flesh (and I have a lot—sin and actual), all of us will struggle with one of these, or both, randomly. Thank you, Steve.

We have to be repeatedly encouraged and reminded to do all God commands us. We tend to do *less than all*, living the Christian life haphazardly and lightly, being easily distracted and diverted by the world. We must do *all* God commands us, not less.

"So, Moses came and called the elders of the people and set before them all these words that the LORD had commanded

him. All the people answered together and said, 'All that the LORD has spoken we will do'" (Exodus 19:7-8 ESV).

"Go therefore and make disciples of all nations, baptizing them in the Name of the Father and of the Son and of the Holy Spirit, teaching them to observe all that I have commanded you. And behold, I Am with you always, to the end of the age" (Matthew 28:19-20 ESV).

We also have to be repeatedly encouraged and reminded to do only what God commands us. We tend to do *more than only* or *other than only,* living the Christian life too busy; being easily entangled by all the ministry-tradition "needs," which are not actually clear commands from God. As we saw earlier, far too many men who pastor and the volunteers are too busy with ministry-traditions, doing more than they should and are consumed by it. As a result, they burn-out. We must do *only* what God commands us, not more, not other than.

Reading through the Old Testament, particularly the Law, it should immediately jump out at us how very specific God is: how His temple should be built: the altar, the colors, the stones, and the fabrics. The offerings: where to offer, how to offer, how much to measure, and when to offer, *"in their prescribed quantities"* (see Numbers 29). God is not vague, that is for sure. He is noticeably clear. What God is basically saying is, *"Do ALL that I command you, not less. Do ONLY what I command you, not more, not other than."* Essentially, *Sola Scriptura*–Scripture alone for faith and practice. Both the Old and New Testaments show us that God is very clear.

Unauthorized Fire

"Now Nadab and Abihu, the sons of Aaron, each took his censer and put fire in it and laid incense on it and offered unauthorized fire before the Lord, which He had not commanded them. And fire came out from before the Lord and consumed them, and they died before the Lord" (Leviticus 10:1-2 ESV).

First of all, what Nadab and Abihu did was not something evil, otherwise, Moses would not have had to specifically say, *"which God had not commanded them."* We all know that sin and evil are not commanded by God, such as lying or adultery.

During seasons of fasting, it is funny and sad to me that there are so many people posting suggestions on social media about fasting bad behaviors. Are we supposed to fast bad behaviors? After fasting, are these behaviors then magically good? No! We do not fast bad behaviors. We are commanded to stop them completely, not just during special times or seasons. Instead, we fast the things that are not sin or evil in themselves. We fast the things that are good, such as, food, or even sex in marriage (1 Corinthians 7:5).

Second, we were not there in the temple, and the Bible does not tell us the intentions of their hearts. It is possible Nadab and Abihu were not doing whatever they were doing with sinful intentions, but with good intentions.

- They were in the temple—like the buildings many use on Sundays.
- They *"each took his censer and put fire in it and laid incense on it and offered it before the Lord,"*—like serving with good intentions in whatever ministry-tradition.
- The fire *"consumed them,"*—like people who are consumed by all the ministry-traditions they feel they *"need"* to keep going; and
- *"They died,"*—like the folks who burn out and leave the Church or leave the faith.

Third, Leviticus 16:1 simply tells us that the sons of Aaron, referring to Nadab and Abihu, *"drew near before the Lord and died."* They were drawing near before God, which is not a bad thing but even encouraged and commanded. *"Draw near to God..."* (James 4:8 ESV). Except what they were doing was not authorized by God, *"which He had not commanded."* They were doing more than and other than what God commanded.

I do not want to burn out again. As I have shared, I have been consumed with many good things and do not want to go back there. I do not want to offer up *"unauthorized fire."* I do not want to do more than or other than what God commanded. Do you? I do not wish to hear Jesus say:

> *"Well did Isaiah prophecy of you hypocrites, as it is written, 'This people honours Me with their lips, but their hearts are far from Me. In vain do they worship Me, teaching as doctrines the commandments of men.' You leave the commandment of God and hold to the tradition of men"* (Mark 7:6-8 ESV).

Tradition

In order to follow the *All and Only*, to do all God commands and only what God commands, it is imperative that we know what are clearly His commands and what are clearly not; what are His commands versus our good intentions or the ever-growing list of ministry-traditions.

Nothing is wrong with tradition. When my kids were young, before they had their own weekend plans, we had a tradition of Saturday mornings' Dad's Big Breffus. Then we would all go clean out the garage (except for my daughter, who for some reason was always "busy" somewhere else in our home). We would invite everybody and anybody over for Boardwalk Pizza and Wingman Wings and watch the weekly survival tv series! These days, we are hosting the latest Jesus' series with Hebrew National Potlucks! L'Chaim!

How do you do your Thanksgiving turkey? Baked? Grilled? Smoked? Barbequed? Broiled? Boiled? Deep-Fried is the only way we will have it. Not just because it tastes the best and does not monopolize your oven, it is tradition!

Christmastime with our grandchildren is super special! We started a tradition with them decorating the bottom 3 feet of our Christmas Tree because that is all their precious little hands could reach.

On other days where we normally serve or bless each other with special gifts (Birthdays, Valentines, Mother's Day, Father's Day, Anniversaries, and Christmas), we decided that we want to first bless others (1 Peter 3:9) before we bless ourselves. A few weeks ago, on Valentine's Day, we had the joy and blessing of preparing and dropping off a meal for my friend, Mark Taracena, whose wife was recovering from surgery.

You may be thinking of some of your own precious family traditions right now, because they are precious. They are special.

*"Families have certain traditions in the way they celebrate holidays, birthdays, or vacations. Family traditions can be a healthy and positive way to maintain family cohesiveness. Social traditions can help create a sense of belonging within a community. A school may have a tradition that each year the incoming freshmen are escorted to the first football game by the seniors. Following those traditions builds unity and helps maintain social norms. In the religious arena, however, **tradition can blur the line between God's truth and man's invention**, thereby confusing many. Christians should view religious tradition with caution"* (Got Questions Ministries).[2020]

Traditions are special. Certain family members may expect it and even demand it, but traditions are not commands from God (Mark 7:6-8). On tradition and many other things, we might compromise, but with the Word of God we must remain intransigent.

Practical Application Questions:

1. What are some of your family's cherished traditions?

_____

_____

_____

_____

_____

2. How do people react with deviations from tradition?

_____

_____

_____

_____

_____

3. How do people typically treat God's commands? With reverence or indifference?

_____

_____

_____

_____

5. How have we left the commandments of God and held to the tradition of men? (Mark 7:8)

_____

_____

_____

_____

_____

God's Clear Commands (just a few)

We cannot speculate and make up what we do not know. I mean, we can, but we should not. Thank God, He gave us His Word, so we are not left in the dark to figure out what His commands clearly are on our own. Here are a few:

Jesus said the greatest commandment is to love God with all our heart, with all our soul, and with all our mind, and to love our neighbors as—*we already do*—love ourselves (Mark 12:30).

Follow Him (Mark 1:17).

Abide in Him (John 15:4).

Go and make disciples (Matthew 28:18-20).

Be baptized (Matthew 28:19; Acts 2:38)

Keep loving one another, (John 13) earnestly (1 Peter 1:22, 4:8). This command occurs at least 16 times.

Pray with and for one another (1 Timothy 2; James 5:16).

Confess your sins to one another (James 5:16).

Forgive one another at least 490 times (Matthew 18; 2 Corinthians 2; Ephesians 4:2, 32; Colossians 3:13). Even those who ask for forgiveness at the eleventh hour (Luke 23:42-43).

Live in harmony with one another (Romans 12:16, 15:5).

Do not pass judgment on one another (Romans 14:13).

Clothe yourselves with humility toward one another (1 Peter 5:5).

Count others more significant than yourselves (Philippians 2:3).

Look to the interests of others (Philippians 2:4).

Submit to one another (Ephesians 5:21; 1 Peter 5:5).

Be patient with one another (Ephesians 4:2; Colossians 3:13).

Outdo one another in showing honour (Romans 12:10).

Rejoice with one another (Romans 12:15).

Grieve with one another (Romans 12:15).

Bear one another's burdens (Colossians 3:13).

Bear with one another (Galatians 6:2).

Have the same care for one another (1 Corinthians 12:25).

Through love, serve one another (Galatians 5:13).

Be kind and tenderhearted to one another (Ephesians 4:32).

Speak the truth in love (Ephesians 4:15, 25).

Speak to one another with psalms, hymns, and spiritual songs (Ephesians 5:19).

Instruct one another (Romans 15:14; Galatians 6:6).

Admonish one another (Colossians 3:16).

Exhort one another every day (Hebrews 3:13).

Show hospitality to one another without grumbling (1 Peter 4:9).

Stir up one another to love and good works (Hebrews 10:24).

Meet together and encourage one another (Hebrews 10:25).

Welcome one another, as Christ welcomed you (Romans 15:7).

Do this [communion] in remembrance of Christ (1 Corinthians 11:24-25).

Encourage and build up one another (1 Thessalonians 5:11).

Use our spiritual gifts to edify and grow God's people, not a building (Ephesians 4).

When you come together, each one has a hymn, a lesson, a revelation, a tongue, or an interpretation. Let all things be done for building up. (1 Corinthians 14:26 ESV)

Use your gifts to serve one another (1 Peter 4:10).

Quite a list, yes? This is not even all the "one-anothers" in the Bible. Here is a helpful website of the one-anothers: All The "One Another" Bible Verses in One Infographic (overviewbible.com).[21]

According to another website, there are 1,050 commands in just the New Testament alone! [22]ONE THOUSAND FITTEE! Yowza! According to John Piper, there are 1,800 individual commands in the New Testament![23]

Besides God's command to love God and abide in Him, God's command to love our neighbor as ourselves, God's command to care for our families, God's command to work, God's command to go and make disciples, there is a lot of one-anothering to do. Are we doing less than *all* of them? Are we doing anything *other* than we should be? Meaning are we doing other good things that are not commanded, while ignoring the things that are clearly commanded? Are we offering up "*unauthorized fire?*" If we are not even one-anothering one another, should we pat ourselves on the back for all the ministry we are doing?

The one-anothers happen in the context of just doing life together and *"building up the body of Christ"* (Ephesians 4:12 ESV). When did they become no more than performing *"religious acts in a building?"* We sign up for a ministry-tradition, do our time, then check it off our list.

But... are we truly one-anothering one another?

Practical Application Questions:

1. Please. Stop right now. Take some time and take your time to read and reflect on each of the one-anothers slowly and carefully.

_____

_____

_____

_____

_____

2. We are commanded by God's Word to one-another one another. Yet most Sunday mornings are folks sitting in rows facing one direction for 1-2 hours and then go home. Is this your experience? How have we been one-anothering one another?

_____

_____

_____

_____

_____

Love, Not Legalism

Now before we continue, please do not hear what I am not saying. I am not in any way referring to being *"justified by the law"* (Galatians 5:4 ESV). This is not about legalism. Do not allow the devil to deceive you to just brush off the one-anothers because we are supposed to avoid legalism. Avoiding legalism does *not* mean avoiding what God clearly commands.

This is not about attempting to earn our salvation, somehow securing it by our performance, by doing good deeds, by our own merit, or by keeping the law 100% perfectly because, in truth, we cannot. This is what a legalist believes. Legalism is about the law versus a relationship with God from a truly surrendered heart.

Galatians 5:4 is a huge encouragement because we are reminded that we are not and cannot be *"justified by the law."* Our good works and obedience are not *to be* saved but because *we are*! Obedience is not legalism. We are to avoid legalism, not obedience. Our aim should be *"to bring about the obedience of faith for the sake of His Name among the nations"* (Romans 1:5 ESV). We should *"not venture to speak of anything except what Christ has accomplished through me to bring the Gentiles to obedience—by word and deed"* (Romans 15:18) ESV.

This is about obedience from the heart—a truly submitted heart, *not* legalism. As Jesus said, this is about love, because *"If you love Me, you will keep My commandments"* (John 14:15 ESV). This is about *love*, not legalism. If we love Him and our neighbor as ourselves, *"the whole law is fulfilled"* (Galatians 5:14 ESV).

I was discipling a young man who wanted to get more involved with the music ministry-tradition in his church. We also talked about his ongoing struggle to meet with Jesus or even pick up the Bible to read it. Remember: only 9% read the Bible on a daily basis (see chapter 2).

So, I asked him, *"Does God command us to love Him with all our heart? To love His Word and walk with Him daily?"* He answered, *"Yes."* I asked, *"Does God command us to be in music ministry-tradition?"* He could not give an answer. Folks, we are clearly commanded to love God with all our heart, but if we are not meeting with God and walking with Him daily, should we be involved in music ministry-tradition or any ministry-tradition? You cannot give away what you, yourself, do not have. Obedience to God's clear command is first before anything else.

This has been the number one thing I have dealt with in discipling and meeting with men who pastor, committed leaders and volunteers, and *"the rank and file,"* whom one leader condescendingly referred to members of his church. So many people, even leaders and men who pastor, do not meet with God regularly. Remember this sad statistic: 72% said the only time they spend studying the Word is when they are preparing their sermons. Not meeting with Jesus, not drinking from the Fountain; and not feeding their own souls.

So undernourished, drinking from broken cisterns instead of The Fountain of living waters, yet they still think they can adequately lead others? Is this arrogance or ignorance? Only God truly knows. They are pouring out from empty cups. But pouring out what? You cannot pour from an empty cup. You cannot serve from an empty vessel.

You cannot give what you do not have.

"They made me keeper of the vineyards; but my own vineyard I have not kept" (Song of Solomon 1:6 ESV).

"If someone does not know how to manage his own household, how will he care for God's Church?" (1 Timothy 3:5 ESV).

If you are too busy, then guess what? You are too busy. Do all and only God clearly commands. Do not *"leave the commandment of God and hold to the tradition of men"* (Mark 7:8 ESV).

Is your cup empty? Again, there is a Fountain of living waters for you to quench your thirst.

Come to The Fountain and drink.

Pick a verse or four to memorize this week to hear God's voice.
Pray these verses back to God.
Sing to Him a song of reflective worship.

SONG FOR REFLECTIVE WORSHIP
Be Thou My Vision by Mary E. Byrne and Eleanor H. Hull[24]

Be Thou my Vision, O Lord of my heart
Naught be all else to me, save that Thou art
Thou my best Thought, by day or by night
Waking or sleeping, They Presence my Light

Be Thou my Wisdom, be Thou my true Word
I ever with Thee, and Thou with me, Lord
Thou my great Father and I Thy true son
Thou in me dwelling and I with Thee one

Be Thou my Buckler, my Word for the fight
Be Thou my Dignity, Thou my Delight
Thou my soul's Shelter, Thou my high Tow'r
Raise Thou me heav'nward, O Pow'r of my pow'r

Riches I heed not, nor vain empty praise
Thou mine Inheritance, now and always
Thou and Thou only, first in my heart
High King of heaven, my Treasure Thou art

True Light of heaven, when vict'ry is won
May I reach heaven's joys, O bright heav'ns Sun!
Heart of my own heart, whatever befall
Sill be my Vision, O Ruler of all

PRAYER JOURNAL

5. JESUS TIME

"How is your Jesus time?" People who know me know I will ask them this almost every time. Ask my children, and they will tell you this was the number one thing they heard from me as they were growing up and even to this day. My son, Harrison, said yesterday that even his friends would ask him teasingly because apparently, I asked his friends, too. So, how is yours?

A Non-Negotiable Priority

As El Guapo might say, *"There are a plethora"* of ministry-traditions. But, if we are neglecting His clear commands, we should not be doing what is not commanded. Especially if we are not obeying the first clear command to love God with ALL our hearts, ALL our souls, ALL our minds, and ALL our strength! (Mark 12:30-31 ESV). All means all.

The first and obvious way is spending time with God for God, Himself. This is for every Christian, young or old, veteran or new: you should not be involved with anything if your Jesus Time is not your first priority, much less even a thought.

People will wake up early, get ready, wash up, get dressed, and drive for a meeting. They will do all that work to drink from broken cisterns (see chapter 3). But to spend time with Jesus? To drink at The Fountain? He does not ask us to get ready or clean ourselves. Remember the fishermen along the shores of Galilee (Mark 1:16-20)? Jesus called them but did not say they had to clean themselves. They just had to come as they were. He would do the cleansing. They just had to die to their old life and leave it behind. He would give them new life, abundant life!

This is the easiest thing that God asks of us. Do you know how easy and simple this is? We do not have to get washed, get dressed and drive somewhere. We do not even have to get out of bed to spend time with Jesus.

I remember the first time I met Darrin Deichmann. We were in his house on Koenigstein Avenue. Despite having just met, he asked me, *"How is your quiet time* (with Jesus in His Word)?" What surprised me was that he did not ask with judgment or as a "*gotcha!*" nor was he trying to one-up me. Here was a brother who genuinely cared about my spiritual well-being. It was the first time anyone asked me that. And sadly, it is also one of the few times I have ever been asked, though I have asked many to please ask. Darrin, thank you for asking.

When you wake, what are your first thoughts? To check Twitter, email, or the news? To see how many likes you received on social media? To catch the latest post or picture of those you are following on Instagram? Or are your first anxious thoughts of your dog's bladder?

Or prayerfully, your first thoughts are like David, who said, "*As for me, I shall behold Your face in righteousness. When I awake, I shall be satisfied with Your likeness*" (Psalm 17:15 ESV). Why were these David's first thoughts when he awoke? Because he knew, "*You* [God] *make known to me the path of life. In Your presence there is fullness of joy. At Your right hand are pleasures forevermore*" (Psalm 16:11 ESV).

When I ask people, "*How is your Jesus Time?*" a lot of them say, "*Could be better.*" Of course, it could be better. Everything we do could always be better. So, I ask again, "*Seriously. How is your Jesus Time?*" And they say, "*Well... I talk with Jesus throughout the day. I'm talking to Him all the time.*" And that is a good thing. We should be talking with Jesus throughout our day. We should be talking with Him all the time. He is, after all, "*with us always*" (Matthew 28:20 ESV). But when I clarify and ask about a *specific* time with Jesus, they sort of say the same thing again, "*Oh, well I talk with Jesus all the time, so...*" as if to justify not needing a specific time.

If you were to ask married men, "*Do you talk with your wife throughout your day?*" Almost all of them will say, "*Yes.*" If you ask for more clarification, "*Do you talk with her in the morning? At breakfast? Before you leave for work? Maybe call her during your lunch break? And then call her for a few minutes during the afternoon lull? On your way home from work, you call from the car? When you get home, you catch up for a bit? Talk at the supper table? Talk together in the living room as you download the day's events? Talk before bed? You talk with her throughout your day?*" Almost all of them will reticently say, "*Umm... yeeeah...?*"

This is a good thing. These are not gotcha questions to trip you up. We should be talking with our wives throughout the day whenever possible. Good husband. Good boy. Pat yourself on the back. Give yourself a high five. Atta boy!

And if you really are doing all that, your wife will probably concur that you call her or text her throughout her day. But what would she say if I ask her, "*Since your husband does such a good job of connecting and communicating with you all day... then he does not need to date you, right?*" And ALL the men will immediately say, "*Uhh yeah, no. Don't ask her that.*"

Why? If husbands are talking with their wives throughout the day, calling her, texting her, seeing how things are going, connecting with her, then why would a man be "scurred" of his wife being asked if they still need to date? Because we all know her answer, Friends. And this is why. There is something about that specific time set aside for intimacy and growing closer to one another. It is so much more than just a catch-up or a drive-by conversation. Even though they may be connecting throughout the day, it is still important to continue dating each other for the purposes of being intimate with one another, discovering more treasures about the other, and continually growing closer to each other.

Jesus Time
is a non-negotiable priority.

In the same way that husbands and wives need to set aside specific time for a one-on-one intimate date, we, as the bride of Christ, must also, in a sense, "date" Jesus. Now, this talk about intimacy with Jesus is probably making some of you men uncomfortable. Though most men think immediately of sex when asked about intimacy, intimacy is far more than sexual. I have heard it said that men will pursue intimacy to have sex. Women will have sex to pursue intimacy.

Robbi and I watched a movie last week. Early in the movie, the husband was venomously shouting, "*We haven't been intimate for two years!*" His wife, more composed but with more potent venom, corrected him. *"No. We haven't slept together for two years. But we haven't been intimate for ten."* Ouch!

What is Intimacy?

After telling my kids since they were little, Harrison gets it now. At only 21-years-old *today* (Happy Birthday, Bubba!), he understands what too many men, or more accurately, "grown boys," do not understand or just simply ignore. I am a proud Dad to hear from his own lips that he is actively not pursuing anything "romantical" because he knows that romance is inevitable. It will happen. Instead, he is purposefully trying to get to know gals objectively before anyone's heart is engaged and subjective feelings cloud objectivity and clear thinking.

Romance and sexual intimacy are awesome and amazing. Even inspiring. But besides romance and sexual intimacy, and more importantly, **before** romance and sexual intimacy, there must be intellectual intimacy, emotional intimacy, experiential intimacy, and spiritual intimacy, and there must be a legitimate wedding.

Intellectual intimacy is sharing our beliefs, perspectives, values, and worldview without fear of conflict or rejection. It is getting to know someone objectively first before emotions take over. Emotional intimacy is sharing our emotions, fears, dreams, desires, doubts, and disappointments with each other. Then, there is experiential intimacy in which we share experiences that become private jokes and precious memories.

In the beginning of our friendship, Robbi Gail and I talked about our love for cooking. She showed me her kitchen drawer where she kept all her spices, to which I mentioned how I also kept mine in a drawer, except in categorical and alphabetical order. She then innocently said what made her blush immediately after saying it, *"Well wouldn't it be funny when one day our spices would mingle?"* Hmm... there you go—a shared experience of what is now no longer a private joke.

The last and most important is spiritual intimacy. Transparency with shortcomings. Confessing sins. Forgiving quickly. Praying together. Worshiping together. Studying together. Growing in Christ together. Serving together. Ministering together. If possible, going on missions together. This is key. This is significant.

So, what is intimacy? *Knowing* intellectually, emotionally, experientially and spiritually. *And being known* emotionally, intellectually, experientially, and spiritually.

To Know Intimately and Be Intimately Known

So, how is your Jesus Time? To put it simply, Jesus Time is spending time with Jesus: time specifically set aside for intimacy and growing closer, to know Him intimately and be intimately known by Him (John 17:3). In other words: to enjoy and be enjoyed because, *"I am my Beloved's, and my Beloved is mine"* (Song of Solomon 6:3 ESV). It is "the hub of the wheel" (see chapter 3), the time set aside to drink from The Fountain for nourishment and sustenance, drinking from The Fountain as an end in Itself. As we drink, our cup then overflows and pours out into others. We follow the example of Jesus, Himself, *"rising very early in the morning, while it was still dark, He departed and went out to a desolate place, and there He prayed"* and had communion with Abba (Mark 1:35 ESV).

How do we spend time with Jesus?
* Hear His Voice
* Commune with Him
* Sing to Him

Hear His Voice

The Bible is the only tangible item we have that represents God Himself. It is the most authentic representation of God's voice. So, reading It is the most direct way to access the very heart and voice of God. God wants to speak with you. He does speak to you. Do you want to hear Him? Open your Bible and hear His voice.

Time with Jesus in His Word is more than just Bible reading. Bible reading is good. It is necessary because we need a healthy diet of God's Word. But anyone can read the Bible. Even the devil and demons know the Bible better than any of us.

Being in His Word is more than just Bible study. Studying God's Word is also essential and part of a healthy diet. We should know It well. We need to know It well. But again, anyone can study the Bible, even non-Christians.

Martin Luther studied and knew the Bible more than most men, even knowing the original languages of the texts, and this was all *before* he became a Christian. As a non-Christian, he read and studied God's Word more than most Christians. And the devil and demons knew It even better than he. Anyone can read and study the Bible.

We need to read God's Word. We must study God's Word. Even though it is good and important to read and study the Bible, it is not enough. I am not saying the Bible is not enough, but just reading and studying It is insufficient because anyone can read and study the Bible and still not have an intimate and personal relationship with Jesus.

Today, I was so excited to see a good friend I had not seen for awhile. I sat across our kitchen island from this young man who sincerely loves his Bible, spends hours reading and highlighting verses, and cross-referencing them with other verses. His Bible is a panoply of colors as almost every verse is highlighted with the different colored highlighters he carries with him. But today, my heart broke as he shared with me where all his reading and studying has taken him—the message of God's redemption and reconciliation through Jesus was not for him. He said, "*God is still God and Jesus is still Saviour,*" just not his.

Jesus Time is more than just reading and studying the Bible as anyone can read and study the Bible. Spending time with Jesus in His Word is hearing God speak to you through His Word.

Now, please do *not* hear what I am *not* saying. I am not referring to how many people wrongly think, "*My interpretation of these verses is this because this is what they say to me.*" It is very much like the inanity of people who say, *"This is my truth."* My truth?!? When I was talking about this with Harrison, he said, *"This is so close-minded."* He is correct because truth is truth, regardless of if we feel some type of way, who we are, or what our culture thinks. Reality is reality. Gravity is true and real. Gravity does not care about your feelings or whether you are a Christian or a non-Christian, brown or white, tall or short, fat or skinny, young or old, popular or unknown, poor or rich, blue-collar or white-collar, male or female. Even dead or alive, gravity does not distinguish. Truth, like gravity, just is.

Listen. Most people will *say* they want the truth, but they do not really want the truth. They want to be constantly reassured that what they *believe* is the truth. But Jesus does not say, *"This is what I Am saying to just you and no one else."* No. He clearly says, *"I have come to bear witness to The Truth"* to everyone (John 18:37 ESV).

Jesus Time is an encounter with the living God and engaging with Him. It is hearing God speak to you through His Word and letting His Word speak to your life as you seek out His. Let His Word speak to your thoughts as you read and meditate on His thoughts. Hear His Word speak to your heart as you hear what is on His heart. Let God speak to you through His Word to your situation, your needs, your confusion, your doubts, your struggles, your anguish, your desperation, your fears, even your dreams, your aspirations, and your joys. Again, the goal is to know intimately and be intimately known, to enjoy and be enjoyed. This is intimacy with God.

Dating your spouses is more than talking about the kids, finances, and house projects. More than anything and above anything, dating your spouses is seeing, knowing and enjoying them more. Jesus Time is learning things about ourselves and how to grow in our Christian walk. But it is more than just about practical doing. We jump so quickly to, *"What do I need to do? How do I apply this practically?"* Nothing wrong with that. But, more than anything, above everything, Jesus Time is seeing *and* knowing *and* loving *and* enjoying Jesus more.

God's Word is important because more than His commands and instructions, He is revealing more of Himself to us, His thoughts toward and about us, His desires for us, and His love for us. And frankly, it is far more important for us to hear God's Words, than for Him to hear ours.

Commune With Him

I am not saying that God does not want to hear our words. He does want to hear our words. He even commands it. He commands us to *"pray that you may not enter into temptation"* (Mark 14:38 ESV), *"pray at all times in the Spirit"* (Ephesians 6:18 ESV), and *"pray without ceasing"* (1 Thessalonians 5:17 ESV). We are also commanded to *"pray for one another"* (James 5:16 ESV), *"pray for kings and all who are in high positions"* (1 Timothy 2:1-2 ESV) and pray for our city (Jeremiah 29:7 ESV). God wants to hear our prayers, and *"His ears are open to our prayers"* (1 Peter 3:12).

Back in February, we were able to participate in a city-wide prayer-walk for the city of Vacaville, CA. It was exciting and wonderful to gather with my baby sister, Meliza, her family, and hundreds of people for prayer. We  met at the Maximum Fitness parking lot with the plan to prayer-walk through the city ending at the police department where we would pray for the city government and police department. A couple of highlights were seeing and hearing my sister praying for each of the businesses and restaurants she passed. It was also encouraging to see and hear her husband, Chris, read aloud over the city the wisdom from Proverbs, and my young nephew, Truson, read aloud from 1 Timothy. We need more of this happening, especially since we are commanded to *"be devoted to the public reading of Scripture"* (1 Timothy 4:13 ESV).

People usually refer to prayer-time with Jesus as being in prayer meetings or city-wide prayer-walks, which are wonderful. Yes, we should gather to pray together in prayer groups and city-wide prayer-walks. It is sad that the prayer meeting is typically the least attended meeting for most churches. You all go to the worship night because the band is *fire* or *gas* or whatever the new slang is. I cannot keep up. You go to listen to the hipster preacher because he is funny, entertaining, and you like his *steez*. But how popular is Jesus? It makes me wonder because to be honest, even though we saw hundreds of people come out for the prayer-walk, I only saw a few people actually praying. I could be wrong. I know that many people are uncomfortable praying out loud, just as they do not want to sing out loud.

But let me ask: when was the last time you prayed to God by yourself when no one was around to hear you pray except for Jesus? When was the last time that you specifically set aside that time to talk with Jesus? When was the last time you had communion with Jesus? Spending time with Jesus in prayer is communion. Communion is intimacy. It is communicating deeply, as *"deep cries out to deep"* (Psalm 42:7 ESV), like a bride expressing a deep desire to know and enjoy her groom and be known and enjoyed by Him. So:

- Hear His Voice
- Commune with Him Through Prayer and...

Sing to Him

Last year on the anniversary of 9/11, we went up to Fort Collins to worship Jesus in the park. I am no expert in counting crowds, but I was told there were about four thousand people there. It was awesome to hear so many voices uninhibited and singing with abandon to our King! I love hearing God's people sing! It is one of my greatest thrills that amps me up, so I really dislike when leaders and bands drown out God's people with their amplified voices and instruments, no different than the world's concerts.

Aside from Bible reading, Bible study, prayer meetings, and prayer walks, people will also refer to spending time with Jesus as listening to worship songs or singing to Him in Sunday morning gatherings or large worship concerts in a park or stadium. And we should listen to worship songs—*biblically sound* worship songs—and we should be singing them together with a small group or a large crowd. But how about just you and Jesus?

Perhaps you have said in the past that you are uncomfortable worshiping aloud in a group because you do not think you are a good singer. Okay. Okay. I get that, just like some people are not comfortable praying out loud in a group.

So, when was the last time you sang a song to Him by yourself when no one was around to hear you except for Jesus? How is your personal time of worshiping Jesus?

There are many passionate people out there saying, "*Love is not a feeling*." They are partly true. Love is not only a feeling, but it is not *not* a feeling. Love is more than a feeling, but that does not mean it is not a feeling at all. While worship is definitely more than a song, that does not mean it is not a song at all.

I can still see and hear my friend Steve Snyder singing a hymn or humming a chorus walking around Grace Community Church in Franklin Lakes, NJ. I thought to myself then, "*This guy must sing to Jesus during his time alone with Him because he is always singing even when just sitting in his office or walking down to the fellowship hall.*" My son-in-law, Micah, is the same, spontaneously anywhere crying out with a song to Jesus, kind of like Moses' brother Aaron during the Passover scene in that famous movie from the 1950s. Steve's and Micah's singing to Jesus just by themselves is evidence of a very intimate relationship with their Saviour.

Meeting on the Kissing Ground

We are given a glimpse of worship in the Book of Revelation when we are told what the angels, living beings, and we along with people from every tongue and tribe will be doing for eternity. The word John uses in Revelation for worship is: "προσκύνησον" from προσκυνέω (pronounced pros-koo-neh'-o).

Proskynéō (from 4314 /*prós* "towards" and *kyneo*, "*to kiss*")—to *worship*, ready "to fall down/prostrate oneself to adore on one's knees" (*DNTT*); to "do obeisance" (*BAGD*). ["The basic meaning of 4352 (*proskynéō*), in the opinion of most scholars, is to *kiss*... 4352 (*proskyneō*) has been (metaphorically) described as "**the kissing-ground**" between believers **(the Bride) and Christ (the heavenly Bridegroom).** While this is true, 4352 (*proskynéō*) suggests the willingness to make all necessary physical *gestures of obeisance.*] (HELPS Word-Studies from The Discovery Bible).[25]

If you have noticed, every chapter in this book ends with a Song for Reflective Worship. Why? Because all of life is to worship God and everything culminates in the worship of God as Revelations shows us. Even our Jesus Time.

Personal worship of Jesus in our time with Him is just simply that—singing to Him a song in obeisance, which is adoration with a kiss toward the One Whom you love and adore and revere. It is meeting on the kissing-ground with the One you love with a song of reflection of all He has revealed about Himself to you from His Word and by His Spirit through prayer.

With as much as our finite minds are able, we acknowledge and ascribe to God all His majesty and worth and power and beauty, and all the glory and honour and praise due Him! And with all our affections, desiring and delighting and boasting and treasuring in Him and all His attributes above all things and everything and anything!

"So, our spiritual worship is to come to God each day and say: "O God, there is nothing that I want more than to approve what is most worthy, and value what is most valuable, and treasure what is most precious and admire what is most beautiful and hate what is most evil and abhor what is most ugly. I reckon myself dead to all that is unspiritual and worldly and deadening to my soul. Renew me, O my God. Awaken spiritual capacities of right assessment."[26]

And then we say, "And take me, body and soul, and make me the instrument of Your glory in the world. Let the renewal You are working from within show on the outside. This is my spiritual worship. To show the world that You are my all-satisfying treasure" (John Piper).[27]

Practical Application Questions:

1. How is your Jesus Time? What is your typical morning routine?

_____

_____

_____

_____

_____

2. *"My own vineyard I neglected."* (Song of Solomon 1:6) What is God saying to you here?

_____

_____

_____

_____

_____

3. IF you are a Christian, your Jesus Time should be the most non-negotiable priority in your life. I encourage you to take some time right now to slowly and contemplatively reread these short verses: Psalm 16:11, Psalm 17:15, and Mark 1:35. What does this reveal of Jesus' character? What did you "hear" from the Holy Spirit?

_____

_____

_____

_____

_____

4. How are you getting to know Jesus more and being known by Him more? What is your plan to get to know Him more and be known by Him more?

_____

_____

_____

_____

_____

Remember that exhausting list of ministry-traditions? So, you do not have to flip back to that page; here you go:

Sunday morning programs. Sunday evening programs. Wednesday evening programs. Setup-Teardown-Clean up-*Repeat*. Men's ministry. Women's ministry. Marriage ministry. Singles ministry. Single Moms' ministry. Single Dads' ministry. Divorce ministry. Counseling ministry. Children's ministry. Vacation Bible School. Youth ministry. College ministry. Senior ministry. Music ministry. Drama ministry. Coffee shop ministry. Bagel bar ministry. Hospitality ministry. Greeting ministry. Benevolence ministry. Child-care. Sunday Schools. New Members Foundations Classes. Community outreaches. Guest services. Guest follow-ups. Building cleaning. Building maintenance. Remodeling. Renovations. Upgrades. Raising funds. Distributing funds. Administrative functions. Meetings. Meetings. And more meetings! Paying the bills—mortgage or rent, utilities, supplies, upkeep and replacements, salaries, etc. Then there is all the "needed" advertising for the church. Marketing. Merchandising. Branding. Photography. Website. Social media. And all the prep and study time (And remember that website that listed even more?!)

"Merely because we are busy, or even skilled, at doing something does not necessarily mean that we are getting anything accomplished. The question must always be asked: is it worth doing? And does it get the job done? This is a question that should be posed continually to the... activity of the church. Are our efforts to keep things going fulfilling the great commission of Christ?" (Robert Coleman).[28]

We are busy, Friends. Too busy. And if you are too busy, you know what that means? It means you are too busy. We not only need to ask if all these ministry-traditions are worth doing, but are they commands from God? Or are they no more than man-made traditions?

Time with Jesus is imperative. Time with Jesus means life or death. We need living water. It is a command from God because He knows what we truly need, what we desperately need, Himself.

While they are good, nothing on the list above is commanded by God. Therefore, we cannot definitively say they are necessary. But we can say from experience that they are lots of work, time-consuming, energy-draining, resource-depleting, properly hard, and mostly result in burnout, relational breakdown, spiritual problems, and discouragement. But there is good news, Friends. Incredibly good news!

Before you rush into the next chapter, please spend some time with Jesus right now. *"Seek His Presence continually"* (1

Chronicles 16:11 ESV). Drink at The Fountain of living waters. I promise you, there is no better investment of your time and no greater return.

Pick a verse or five to memorize this week to hear God's voice.

Pray these verses back to God.

Sing to Him a song of reflective worship.

SONG FOR REFLECTIVE WORSHIP
Give Me Jesus by Fanny Crosby[29]

Take the world, but give me Jesus
All its joys are but a name
But His love abideth ever
Through eternal years the same

Take the world, but give me Jesus
Sweetest comfort of my soul
With my Saviour watching o'er me
I can sing though billows roll

Take the world, but give me Jesus
Let me view His constant smile
Then throughout my pilgrim journey
Light will cheer me all the while

Take the world, but give me Jesus
In His cross my trust shall be
Till, with clearer, brighter vision
Face to face my Lord I see

Oh, the height and depth of mercy
Oh, the length and breadth of love
Oh, the fullness of redemption
Pledge of endless life above!

PRAYER JOURNAL

6. JESUS BUILDS. WE MAKE DISCIPLES.

In Matthew 16, before He told His disciples to go and make disciples, Jesus said, "*I will build My Church.*" (Matthew 16:15 ESV). Do not miss this. Whom did Jesus say will build His Church? He said *He* would build His Church. *Jesus* builds.

> "*What I want to drive home here is the triumphant authority of this promise. World Missions is not ultimately dependent on human initiative or human wisdom or human perseverance. It is ultimately dependent on the power and wisdom and faithfulness of the risen and living Christ to keep this promise: "I will build My church." Not, "You will build My church." Or "Missionaries will build My church." Or "Pastors will build My church." But "I will build My church… Yes, missionaries are crucial. Pastors and elders are crucial. But we are not ultimate. Christ is ultimate. "I will build My church." One missionary plants. Another missionary or pastor waters. Yes. But Christ gives the growth (1 Corinthians 3:6). CHRIST builds the church. Church planting and church establishing is supernatural work, or it is not the church that gets built, but only a human organization*" (John Piper).[30]

This is good news, Friends! Jesus builds His Church. Not me, not you, nor missionaries, nor men who pastor. Jesus said that He Himself would build His Church. We ourselves, *"like living stones are being built up as a spiritual house, to be a holy priesthood, to offer spiritual sacrifices acceptable to God through Jesus Christ"* (1 Peter 2:5 ESV).

Did you catch that? We *"are being built up."* We are being built up by God Who began His work in us. And He is completing His work through us as we are building up one another. We are being built up by God and as we build up each other, working out our salvation with fear and trembling.

In Philippians 2:12, Paul is not only speaking to each one but to all the Philippians when he says, "*therefore my Beloved* (ἀγαπητοί plural) *as you have always obeyed* (ὑπηκούσατε plural)... *work out your own* (ἑαυτῶν plural) *salvation...*" In other words, *"as **y'all** have always obeyed, work out **your guys's** salvation."* Please forgive the poor grammar. I knows my editors would like for me to write "more better," but you get the point, yes? Paul's instructions are for each of us to individually work out our salvation, and for all of us as a community, as a family, to work it out together.

We are also not building up a literal building as *"the Most High does not dwell in houses made by hands, as the prophet says"* (Acts 7:48 ESV). *"The God Who made the world and everything in it, being Lord of heaven and earth, does not live in temples made by man"* (Acts 17:24 ESV).

We *"are being built up as a spiritual house."* We *are* a spiritual house. *We* are Church. Jesus is building His Church, as He said He would.

The Gospel Will Reach the World

> *"And this <u>Gospel</u> of the kingdom <u>will be proclaimed throughout the whole world</u> as a testimony <u>to all nations</u>, and then the end will come"* (Matthew 24:14 ESV).

God says the Gospel will reach the whole world, meaning every nation, or ἔθνεσιν from ἔθνος, meaning ethnic people groups with cultural and linguistic distinctions. These people groups usually refer to unbelieving gentiles or non-Jews. The cultural and linguistic distinctions make it difficult for the Gospel to spread naturally from one group to another, like from California to Texas. Even though there are vast differences — political, socio-economical, pandemical: mask/no-mask, vax/no vax — between Hollywood and Houston, L.A. and Laredo, San Francisco and San Antonio, or Compton and Corpus Christi, it is not hard for the Gospel to be shared and spread between these places.

Regardless of the distinctions, God said the Gospel WILL reach every people group. Therefore, it will. If our goal is to reach every person, we have already failed because in the time it took to read this sentence, thousands of people have already died. We will never keep up with the world's population growth rate as that changes every day, every minute. But the number of people groups remains the same. The amazing, good news of that is our task, our mission of reaching every people group is finishable, especially every unreached people group, where there is no indigenous disciple-making movement among them. It is doable. It can be done!

And it will be done because this is a clear and absolute promise from God. It will happen because He will accomplish all His purpose (Isaiah 46:10) and *"all authority in heaven and on earth has been given to* [Him]*"* (Matthew 28:18 ESV) *"and the gates of hell shall not prevail"* (Matthew 16:18 ESV). Hallelujah! It will be proclaimed to every nation, every people group, including all the unreached people groups. And we can trust this Word. God said it. It is written. It will be done! How?

Holy Ghost Power

"You will receive power when the Holy Spirit has come upon you, and you will be My witnesses in Jerusalem and in all Judea and Samaria, and to the end of the earth" (Acts 1:8 ESV).

How will the Gospel reach the world? We will receive power from God's Holy Spirit. Another promise from God. We WILL receive power. Woohoo! Who does not want power?! But power for what? For our own purposes? For our own conveniences? To be healthy and wealthy? To live an easy life and retire comfortably? No! We *will* receive power to be His witnesses, and not just in our close surroundings in which we feel safe because it is known and familiar. We will be His witnesses to the ends of the earth, to the darkest and hardest and poorest and most unreached and unengaged places of the world.

God's Reconciliation Message

We will receive Holy Ghost power to be His witnesses to the world.

"Therefore, if anyone is in Christ, the new creation has come: The old has gone, the new is here! All this is from God, Who reconciled us to Himself through Christ and gave us the

ministry of reconciliation: that God was reconciling the world to Himself in Christ, not counting people's sins against them. And He has committed to us the message of reconciliation. We are therefore Christ's ambassadors, as though God were making His appeal through us. We implore you on behalf of Christ, be reconciled to God" (2 Corinthians 5:17-20 ESV).

"Repentance for the forgiveness of sins should be proclaimed in His Name to all nations..." (Luke 24:47 ESV).

"But rise and stand upon your feet, for I have appeared to you for this purpose, to appoint you as a servant and witness to the things in which you have seen Me and to those in which I will appear to you, delivering you from your people and from the Gentiles—to whom I Am sending you to open their eyes, so that they may turn from darkness to light and from the power of Satan to God, that they may receive forgiveness of sins and a place among those who are sanctified by faith in Me" (Acts 26:16-18 ESV).

As witnesses with Holy Ghost power, we are in Christ, new creations. We can testify that *"the old has gone, the new is here! All this is from God, Who reconciled us to Himself through Christ!"* Not only did God reconcile us to Himself and forgave us our sin, but He also gave to us and has committed to us this ministry and message of reconciliation, which is *"repentance for the forgiveness of sins"* (Luke 24:47 ESV).

- Jesus said He would build His Church.
- The Gospel will be preached to all people groups.
- We will receive power from the Holy Spirit.
- He gave to us and has committed to us the message of repentance, forgiveness of sins and reconciliation to God.
- We are to be His ambassador-witnesses in His Name to all people groups to the ends of the earth.

Thus far, this is all God's doing in reaching the world. We are receiving and being but not actually doing yet. What are we supposed to do? While Jesus is building His Church, aside from the ministry of building up the body of Christ by one-anothering one another, what has He commanded us to do to reach the world?

Go. Make. Teach.

He gave and committed to us the ministry and message of reconciliation to be ambassador-witnesses in His Name to all people groups. What are we to do as ambassadors? Ambassadors go. Where? Well, they do not go home. They go to the nations.

> "*Go therefore and <u>make disciples of all nations</u>, baptizing them in the name of the Father and of the Son and of the Holy Spirit, <u>teaching them to observe all that I have commanded you</u>. And behold, I Am with you always, to the end of the age*" (Matthew 28:19-20 ESV).

Friends, I get it that going is a sacrifice. Just one to two centuries ago, missionaries would go knowing they may never see or even hear from family or friends again. Only a few short decades ago, we had to wait a few weeks to receive news from around the world. And international charges for phone calls were extremely expensive. I know. Even calls to and from Nebraska and New Jersey cost an arm and leg! Know that, too. Going was and still is a sacrifice, but with today's technology we are able to speak with and even see our loved ones everyday if we wish. And even for free! In most cases, we can hop on a plane and see them face to face within 24 hours. So, yes, going is a sacrifice, but not as much as it used to be just a little while ago.

So, go. Do not stay. Make disciples. Do not keep it all to yourself. Teach. Do not remain just a learner. Go. Make. Teach. So simple. Much simpler than the ever-growing, never-ending, cost-inflating list of Church ministry-traditions which are a lot of work, time-consuming, energy-draining, resource-depleting, properly hard, and just downright exhausting.

So, why do we do it? Rehoboam added to his father Solomon's yoke because he wanted to make it even heavier (1 Kings 12 and 2 Chronicles 10)? Why do we add to Jesus' yoke? Do we want to make it heavier? Why are we taking His job? We need to honestly answer this question: is what I am doing a clear command from Scripture or just a man-made tradition? Is this a command from God or just how I grew up seeing it done?

We clearly see in His Word that Jesus said that *He* would build His Church (Matthew 16:15). He never commanded or instructed us to do it. Therefore, we might conclude that we get busy building and marketing our churches because *"This is the way it is done. This is the way it has always been done."* Man-made ministry-traditions.

Jesus did not command it. It is exhausting and produces more Church transfer growth than actual growth, and the results are more and more burnout. He said His yoke is easy, but we ignore that and bulldoze through with our agenda from traditions, and we make His yoke hard. We make burdensome what Jesus said is not burdensome. We complicate what should be simple. Busy and burned-out, but no actual disciple-making happening.

"Why is it that we see so little disciple-making taking place in the church today? Do we really believe that Jesus told His early followers to make disciples but wants the twenty-first-century church to do something different? None of us would claim to believe this, somehow, we have created a church culture where the paid ministers do the "ministry," and the rest of us show up, put some money in the plate, and leave feeling inspired or "fed." We have moved so far away from Jesus' command that many Christians don't have a frame of reference for what disciple-making looks like."[31]

"We expect our church leaders to create some sort of disciple-maker campaign where we sign up, commit to participating for a few months, and then cross the Great Commission off our list. But making disciples is far more than a program. It is the mission of our lives. It defines us. A disciple is a disciple maker."[32]

It was good, yet really sad, to catch up with an old friend at a baby shower. He mentioned that he was part of a weekly discipleship group with two other guys. But this is the sad part: there was no desire whatsoever to start meeting with other men because he is "*too busy working*" (30 hours, he said later in the conversation) "*and taking care of the lawn*" (because they have a very nice lawn). Are you kidding me? What kind of discipleship program is this? After a year, he does not know that the command is to "*go and make disciples*," not "*go sit in a class*" and check it off.

Making disciples is far more than a program. It is the mission of our normal everyday lives. I have challenged my children to initiate Jesus in everyday regular conversations. They do not have to wait for their teachers to bring it up and ask a question. Same with discipleship. We do not have to wait for the men who pastor to come up with a new program for discipleship. Just be discipled. Make disciples. It is not that difficult. We all know how to do it.

I remember a friend who said he did not know how to meditate. I asked him how much time he watches Sports Center and how much of his thoughts are about the Redskins, now the Washington Football Team (smh). But he *did* know how to meditate because he was already meditating on his beloved Redskins all throughout football season! ALL of us know how to meditate because we all meditate on all the things we love.

Same with discipleship. We do not need to wait for men who pastor to come up with a discipleship class or program because we all know how to do it. People are so quick to share their knowledge, experience, and "expertise" on fixing a car, preparing a certain dish, or resolving a conflict. You know these people, yes? I am encouraging my cousin to make disciples by telling him it is the same as when he took me climbing—instructing me what to look for and look out for, where to grab, where to place my feet, etc. You know what that is? Discipleship! It is being one or two steps ahead in the path or climb and telling the person following you where to step or not step; what to do, how to do, what not to do, when to do... "*Watch me as I reach for this rock. You do the same. Grab this rock here. Do what I did.*" OR "*Look out! Don't step in that poop. Don't do what I just did.*" It really is that simple. Follow me as I follow Jesus (1 Corinthians 11:1).

How is our government's proficiency in science? Though some deny or ignore, we all saw how covid revealed, or more accurately, exposed how "scientific" our government really is. But did you know that a recent study by them found that people who go fishing actually catch more fish than those who do not go fishing? Like, literally! So, shall we go fishing and make disciples?

Now, *Jesus* will build His Church. His simple command to us is to go and make disciples. And He Himself showed us how to do it. He chose twelve. And then He poured Himself to three. His plan was simple and is simple. May we K.I.S.S., please? Why? Because Jesus kept it simple. He had a simple plan.

Keep It Simple Saint!

Practical Application Questions:

1. Jesus said He will build His Church. How is that good news?

_____

_____

_____

_____

_____

2. Why is it that we see so little disciple-making taking place in the Church today?

_____

_____

_____

_____

_____

SONG FOR REFLECTIVE WORSHIP
I Will Go by FG Burroughs[33]

I will go in the strength of the Lord
To the work He has giv'n me to do
In the strength that is mighty to save
To the field here the lab'rers are few

I will go where He leads
In my weakness His pow'r I shall know
All things, by His grace, I can do
In the strength of the Lord, I will go

I will go at His gentle command
Tho' i know not the way of His choice
But the Lord knoweth me by my name
So, I'll follow my kind Shepherd's voice

I will go where He leads
In my weakness His pow'r I shall know
All things, by His grace, I can do
In the strength of the Lord, I will go

I will go in the strength of the Lord
And no evil shall cause me to fear
Thro' green pastures, or thro' death's dark vale
I will go with my Comforter near

I will go where He leads
In my weakness His pow'r I shall know
All things, by His grace, I can do
In the strength of the Lord, I will go

I will go in the panoply clad
And undaunted by mightiest foe
For no weapon can pierce faith's strong shield
In the strength of the Lord, I will go

I will go where He leads
In my weakness His pow'r I shall know
All things, by His grace, I can do
In the strength of the Lord, I will go

PRAYER JOURNAL

7. JESUS' SIMPLE PLAN: AIM SMALL

These days I need more sleep. A lot more, like maybe 6-7 hours of sleep. But when I was younger, only needing 3-4 hours of sleep, and still able to run a-million-miles-a-minute, man oh man, we all had big visions back then! Visions of reaching all the *"Runners for the Redeemer"* or all the *"Snowboarders for the Saviour."* You get the picture? We even held a *"McLympics Weekend"* to reach all *"McDonald's for Messiah!"* Yeah... we had big visions, as Acts 2:17 tells us. And with big visions, you shoot big. Go big or go home. That is what they say, yes?

A common phrase you may hear at a shooting or archery range is, *"Aim small. Miss small."* Meaning, if you aim big, you will probably miss your target. But if you aim small, you will hit your target. So, *"aim small."*

During Jesus' day, the population of Galilee was about 200,000 to 700,000, spread out among 200 villages. That is a pretty big spread, but using the smallest estimate of 200,000, we can safely guess there may have been an average of around a thousand people in each village, give or take. Without refrigeration, daily fishing was a vital trade. May we assume there would have been at least ten fishermen from each village—ten fishermen to feed one thousand? I am not a fisherman, but that sounds doable. So perhaps at least 2,000 fishermen in the GFU (the Galilean Fishermen's Union)?

2,000 fishermen! As Jesus was walking along the Sea of Galilee, He must have had big visions of a new exciting evangelistic campaign to reach *"All the Fishermen for the Father!"* Is that what we read in Mark 1?

"Passing alongside the Sea of Galilee, He saw Simon and Andrew the brother of Simon casting a net into the sea, for they were fishermen. And Jesus said to them, "Follow Me, and I will make you become fishers of men." And immediately, they left their nets and followed Him. And going on a little farther, He saw James the son of Zebedee and John, his brother, who were in their boat mending the nets. And immediately He

called them, and they left their father Zebedee in the boat with the hired servants and followed Him" (Mark 1:16-20 ESV).

How many did Jesus call? Did He call 2,000 fishermen? He did not seem to have the big vision we have as He only called four. He did not even call the father of James and John or the other hired servants who were there! Nope. He only called four. Four! Aim small?

Jesus left the crowds because *"He had to pass through Samaria"* (John 4:4 ESV). And the only thing we can tell from Scripture is He went there solely to reach one woman.

Four fishermen out of many who were fishing that day. Leaving the crowds to reach one woman. Not thousands or even hundreds. Four. Then one. Aim small. Do we aim small or are we aiming for numbers?

We have an obsession with numbers. Many refuse to admit it, but we make a lot of decisions based on what will draw a crowd. Again, this was not the model of Christ… This is why true life-on-life discipleship is rarely seen" (Francis Chan).[34]

"Men were His method. It all started by Jesus calling a few men to follow Him. This revealed immediately the direction His evangelism strategy would take. His concern was not with programs to reach the multitudes, but with men whom the multitudes would follow. Remarkable as it may seem, Jesus started to gather these men before He even organized an evangelistic campaign or even preached a sermon in public. Men were to be His method of winning the world to God" (Robert Coleman).[35]

"But it was His wish that certain selected men should be with Him at all times and in all places, — His travelling companions in all His wanderings, witnessing all His work, and ministering to His daily needs. And so, in the quaint words of Mark, "Jesus calleth unto Him whom He would, and they came unto Him, and He made twelve, that they should be with Him" (A.B. Bruce, The Training of The Twelve).[36]

"Jesus spent His life investing in a few people. His strategy for reaching all peoples was clear: make disciple-makers among a few people" (David Platt).[37]

"They were unschooled ordinary men" with no standing in the community (Acts 4:13 ESV). No authority from anyone. Not a rabbi among the bunch. Not even with property as they were not allowed to own any, which freed them to go anywhere anytime as they were not tied down to a building.

It all started with investing in just a few unlearned, unordained, mobile nobodies. It was a simple plan. Aim small.

A Paradigm Bomb

This may absolutely blow your mind. This might be, as Tim Keller used in one of his sermons, a "paradigm-bomb!"[38]

In the early '90s, Bob Noyes, the most intentional discipler I know, would meet with me at McDonald's, where I worked at the time. During one of our meetings, Bob shared a picture of disciple-making with the example of a single penny. It was so simple! Just one penny. It was a paradigm-bomb for me, but it was not until now, twenty-nine loooong years later, that Robbi and I did the math on paper and the bomb finally detonated and I am reeling from its effect! Thank you so much, Bob.

A paradigm is an expectation or pattern of something, a model of how we view something. So, a paradigm-bomb is something that blows up that pattern or model. Tim Keller referred to the burning bush in a sermon from Exodus, calling it a paradigm-bomb because naturally, we expect bushes to burn. Well, here is a burning bush that is, um, not burning. Whaaaa..?! Burning, yet not burning?!

BOOM!

We have created models for reaching the lost—our paradigms of planting and marketing churches, multi-ministry-traditions, and large evangelistic outreaches to the masses, even though we see in God's Word that Jesus' model is simpler, yet much larger and more fruitful. He did not come to save just the Jews but all people groups. How? Through His simple plan of discipleship, which blows up all our traditional paradigms and *"religious acts."*

From Just One

For those of you who earn well above the median or national average, first, please thank God every day for it is not you, but *"it is He Who gives you the power to make wealth"* (Deuteronomy 8:18 ESV). Second, please do not rush ahead and totally miss the point of this section which was one of the things that started the whole ball rolling toward writing this book.

Google the median household income before the government-imposed shutdowns in 2020. You will see it was about $63,000 per year. That is around $5,000 per month for a household of one to three persons working and earning.

If, instead of that median income of $5,000, I offered you $11,000, would you accept it? $11,000 for one person to earn for one month. Would that be a good wage for you? Should be. It is more than double the national average for a household.

Or what if I were to offer you one penny for the first day and doubled what you have every day after that for thirty days? Would you accept that instead? Which would you take: $11,000 or the measly penny?

Here is what you would earn from that single penny:

Day 1	1 cent
Day 2	2
Day 3	4
Day 4	8
Day 5	16
Day 6	32
Day 7	64
Day 8	1.28
Day 9	2.56
Day 10	5.12

Day 11	10.24	
Day 12	20.48	
Day 13	40.96	*total after 13 days = only $81.91*
Day 14	81.92	
Day 15	163.84	
Day 16	327.68	
Day 17	655.36	
Day 18	1,310.72	
Day 19	2,621.44	
Day 20	5,242.88	
Day 21	10,485.76	
Day 22	20,971.52	
Day 23	41,943.04	
Day 24	83,886.08	
Day 25	167,772.16	
Day 26	335,544.32	
Day 27	671,088.64	
Day 28	1,342,177.28	
Day 29	2,684,354.56	
Day 30	**5,368,709.12**	

Hmm... $11,000 or $5 million? *Over* $5 million! *"Boom!"* How many people do you think would immediately jump at the $11K without even blinking or thinking? How many would give up on day 13 after only earning less than $100? Yes, taking the penny is slow, like tortoise slow. But! If you are patient, it will prove more fruitful. Dramatically more! 488x more!

You know what? Discipleship is also slow. It is not like piling bricks on top of each other just to make a pile of bricks. Fruit takes time and cultivation. It is a slow process, but more fruitful, and the numbers are more staggering than the example of the penny!

Could you evangelize and win one soul every day for thirty years? Could you?! That would be 365 souls each year! Multiply that by 30 years would be almost 11,000 souls! Woohoo! That would be awesome IF you really could win one soul every day for 30 years. But how many of us could actually do this? And if we could, would we?

Aim Small. Because great things grow from small beginnings—*sic parvis magna*.

Practical Application Questions:

1. We do not encourage others to do what we are not doing or willing to do ourselves. Before leading, we must learn to follow. Who do you respect that may be a good discipler for you, someone from whom you could learn? Ask the Holy Spirit for a posture of humility—you do not know, and teachability—you want to know.

_____

_____

_____

_____

_____

2. Who could you disciple and pass on what you are learning, including the things not to do?

_____

_____

_____

_____

_____

3. What are some of the reasons for the hesitation of being discipled or making disciples?

_____

_____

_____

_____

_____

Could you meet with one person for a year? Would you do that? Helping just *one* person to grow in love with Jesus, know His Word and apply it to everyday life, know how to pray and commune with God, while knowing they are being discipled to pass it on to someone else, to disciple another? Discipling and doing life with one person for one year. And the following year discipling another, while your disciple is also discipling another, and so on with the following year, and the following year, and the following year…

Which would be simpler? Which would prove more fruitful? Evangelizing and saving one soul every day for 30 years? Or:

Year 1	1 disciple-maker of disciple-makers
Year 2	3 disciple-makers of disciple-makers
Year 3	7 disciple-makers of disciple-makers
Year 4	15 disciple-makers of disciple-makers
Year 5	31 disciple-makers of disciple-makers
Year 6	63 disciple-makers of disciple-makers
Year 7	127 disciple-makers of disciple-makers
Year 8	255 disciple-makers of disciple-makers
Year 9	511 disciple-makers of disciple-makers
Year 10	1,023 disciple-makers of disciple-makers
Year 11	2,047 disciple-makers of disciple-makers

Year 12	4,095 disciple-makers of disciple-makers
Year 13	8,191 disciple-makers of disciple-makers
Year 14	16,383 disciple-makers of disciple-makers
Year 15	32,767 disciple-makers of disciple-makers
Year 16	65,535 disciple-makers of disciple-makers
Year 17	131,071 disciple-makers of disciple-makers
Year 18	262,143 disciple-makers of disciple-makers
Year 19	524,287 disciple-makers of disciple-makers
Year 20	1,048,575 disciple-makers of disciple-makers
Year 21	2,097,151 disciple-makers of disciple-makers
Year 22	4,194,303 disciple-makers of disciple-makers
Year 23	8,388,607 disciple-makers of disciple-makers
Year 24	16,777,215 disciple-makers of disciple-makers
Year 25	33,554,431 disciple-makers of disciple-makers
Year 26	67,108,863 disciple-makers of disciple-makers
Year 27	134,217,767 disciple-makers of disciple-makers
Year 28	268,435,455 disciple-makers of disciple-makers
Year 29	536,870,911 disciple-makers of disciple-makers
Year 30	**1,073,741,823 disciple-makers of disciple-makers**

"BOOM!"

Evangelizing and winning one person for Jesus every day = 365 people per year. Keep that up every day for 30 years, 10,950 people! That is not a small insignificant number. That is a whole lot of people. But we need to ask: Are they grounded? Are they mature? Are they equipped? Are they fruitful? Are they even saved?

Simple Discipleship. Life-on-life. Discipling just one person a year and multiplying year after year, after year. If you are patient and if you do not take on more than necessary, it will prove more fruitful. Significantly more! Substantively more! And ALL you are doing is discipling one person. Just one! *Sic parvis magna*—great things grow from small beginnings. How much simpler can it be? Jesus is brilliant! But we all know that.

Let me bring some clarity to the rithmetic before someone says, "*Hold on there, Buckaroo! Those numbers are more than doubling! How in the world does 1 become 3 in year two? How does 3 become 7 in year three?*"

Well, after the first year of discipling one person, you do not just sit back, play pick-up-sticks with your butt-cheeks and watch everything double. You continue to disciple another one. And so on every year after that. For example:

- Year 1: You disciple Johnny (**1**)

- Year 2: You disciple Andy (**2**)
  Your disciple Johnny (1) disciples Jimmy (**3**)

- Year 3: You disciple Petey (**4**)
  Your 1st disciple Johnny (1) disciples Philip (**5**)
  His disciple Jimmy (3) disciples another, Tommy (**6**)
  Your 2nd disciple Andy (2) disciples Bart (**7**)

"*And so on, and so on, and so on…*" for every year you have on earth or even better yet, until Christ returns, "*for that is far better!*" (Philippians 1:23 ESV) Woohoo!

Practical Application Questions:

1. How was this picture of Simple Discipleship a paradigm bomb for you?

_____

_____

_____

_____

_____

2. Is it freeing to know that all you need to do is focus on discipling just one person a year? How is it freeing?

_____

_____

_____

_____

_____

3. I climbed my first 14er with my daughter Sharayah. Actually, with the help of my daughter. It was not an easy climb for my knees and lungs. But with her steady encouragement by my side, sometimes helping me stand back up when I stumbled, telling me now and then where to walk, she helped me up to the peak of the mountain. Who is "helping you up the mountain?" How?

_____

_____

_____

_____

_____

Experienced the same thing in California with my boys, Harrison and SeanThomas, just a few months ago. Every few steps they would look back and ask me, "You good? You good, Dad? You good?" Halfway up Harrison decided to get behind me. I asked him, "Why?" and knew the answer immediately when I almost fell backward, and he helped me keep my balance by putting his hands on my back.

More recently, while in my Covid Communion Room #4225 at Good Samaritan Hospital, SeanThomas was able to visit me, bringing me some food, helping me change, and even washed his old dad's back. Who has your back? How?

_____

_____

_____

_____

_____

Who are you "feeding" and "helping to change?" Who are you "washing with the Word?" How are you doing that?

_____

_____

_____

_____

_____

Now, some of you may be thinking this is all about numbers, all about getting a bigger audience, or a bigger following, but it is quite the contrary. The following section may answer your question or concern. But when you get to Chapter 9 "*So,* Why *Simple Discipleship*,*"* prayerfully, you will see this is really not about the numbers at all. There is a higher and greater motivation. The highest. The greatest. But, before that,

What About the Mass of People Who Followed Jesus?

Aim small. This is in no way saying we ignore or disregard the mass of people, as our Lord did not ignore or disregard them. He did teach and feed the five thousand in Mark 6. And He did it again, but with only four thousand in Mark 8.

We do not discount or push aside any who wish to come and hear about Jesus. All are welcome! No cover charge. No hoops. No TSA. The crowds were not snubbed by Jesus. He welcomed them, taught them, and fed them. But did He purposely seek out crowds? No.

Yes, Jesus came to seek and save the lost (Luke 19:10). But was He seeking lost crowds? Did He plan big events or crusades for the crowds? Did He put together revivals? Was it as depicted in a popular Bible tv series where the disciples are planning, promoting, and preparing a big event for Jesus' Sermon on the mount? On the contrary, the Bible does not show us that at all. The Bible actually tells us that Jesus left the crowds (Matthew 8) and even hid from them (John 8). He would even withdraw because there was a crowd.

"But now even more the report about Him went abroad, and great crowds gathered to hear Him and to be healed of their infirmities but, He would withdraw to desolate places"

"Now the man who had been healed did not know Who it was, for Jesus had withdrawn." Why? *"As there was a crowd in the place"*

Jesus' *"fame spread everywhere"* (Mark 1:28 ESV) after He healed the man with the unclean spirit. *"That evening they brought to Him all who were sick or oppressed by demons"* (Mark 1:32 ESV). The disciples found Jesus and said, *"Everyone is looking for You"* (Mark 1:37 ESV). How did Jesus respond? Did He stay for the crowd? Did He plan an event since everyone was looking for Him? No. Instead, He said, *"Let us leave and go to the next town"* (Mark 1:35-39 ESV). He left.

John the Baptist had no small following. *"All the country of Judea and all Jerusalem were going out to him and were being baptized by him in the river Jordan, confessing their sins"* (Mark 1:5 ESV). That is a massive mass of people—*all* the country of Judea and *all* Jerusalem? Regarding Jesus, Matthew tells us, *"Great crowds followed Him from Galilee and the Decapolis, and from Jerusalem and Judea, and from beyond the Jordan"* (Matthew 4:25 ESV). The Apostle John tells us in John 4:1 that Jesus' following was even bigger than that of the Baptizer. So, what does Jesus do? Verse 3 says, *"He left."* He leaves again?! Here is an even more massive mass, and Jesus leaves?! This is totally the opposite of what Church growth experts today might advise even the Lord.

The Mass Did Not Impress Jesus

People will always be attracted to what is real and genuine, like the crowds who *"got into the boats and went to Capernaum, to look for Jesus"* (John 6:24 ESV). Jesus said people will also be attracted to what will fill their bellies (John 6:26), because they did not see that the signs were supposed to point them to Him. The majority of the crowds were not wanting Jesus but rather what He could do for them or give them. Jesus can be so very useful for our own personal ends.

Today is not any different. Many people come to Jesus *not* for Jesus Himself, but they come for their "promised miracle." They come to have a better life or that they can become more like Him. They come to Jesus so that they will have godly lives, godly marriages, and godly families. Nothing wrong with any of that, but they are not coming to Jesus for Jesus. They are *using* Jesus "to fill their bellies," nothing more. You see, Jesus is so useful.

"Jesus was making and baptizing more disciples than John" (John 4:1 ESV). He then says to His disciples, *"there are some of you who do not believe"* (John 6:64 ESV) and *"after this many of His disciples turned back and no longer walked with Him"* (John 6:66 ESV). Almost everyone left and no longer walked with Him as He turned and asked the twelve, *"Do you want to go away as well?"* (John 6:67 ESV).

Basically, Jesus is saying, *"Crowds come to fill their bellies. The mass seeks for miracles. Some of them do not even believe in Me and only come for 'their' miracle. Almost all of them have turned away and are no longer walking with Me. Do you want to go away as well?"* The crowds did not impress Jesus.

The Mass Were Not Impressed

When it was a miracle they did not like or one that did not benefit them, even the crowds asked Jesus to leave. They were not impressed sometimes. He had just miraculously healed the two demon-possessed men, which should have been the headlines and the focus. But almost like most of the media of our day that disregards the good done by those who have differing views, the crowd focused on the herd of pigs that *"rushed down the steep bank into the sea and were drowned in the sea"* (Mark 5:13 ESV). They focused on the lost pigs, even though they were told everything, *"especially what had happened to the demon-possessed men"* (Matthew 8:33 ESV). They were totally missing the Gospel of the Kingdom that Jesus came to proclaim and *"healing every disease and every affliction among the people,"* (Matthew 4:23 ESV). *"Behold, all the city came out to meet Jesus, and when they saw Him, they begged Him to leave their region"* (Matthew 8:34 ESV).

Very early in the morning before His crucifixion, the mass, now more like a mob stirred up by the religious leaders, was really not impressed with Jesus at all. When asked by the governor three times whom they wanted released, they rejected Jesus each time and chose a murderer instead.

Disciples Before Crowds

Now, there were times when Jesus did preach publicly. *"When Jesus had finished instructing His twelve disciples, He went on from there to teach and preach in their cities… As they went away, Jesus began to speak to the crowds concerning John"* (Matthew 11:1, 7 ESV) But this was *AFTER* He had finished personally instructing His disciples. Disciple-making was His first priority.

Jesus did not chase after crowds or even want the crowds to know Him. He did not market Himself or His ministry. He *"ordered them not to make Him known"* (Matthew 12:16 ESV) *"Then He strictly charged the disciples to tell no one that He was the Christ"* (Matthew 16:20 ESV).

We do not ignore the masses or the crowds, but we do not go after them. We do not chase them or try to sell our church to them. We do as Jesus commands — go and make disciples, not win converts or build an audience to listen to us for 1-2 hours a week. Nor are we commanded to merely be spectators in the audience and nothing more.

Jesus commands us to be continuously making disciples and consistently teaching them to make disciples who will make disciples who will also make disciples. His command continues with, *"teaching them to observe all that I have commanded you"* (Matthew 28:20 ESV).

"Tell the coming generation the glorious deeds of the Lord, and His might, and the wonders that He has done… so that they should set their hope in God and not forget the works of God but keep His commandments." (Psalm 78:4, 7 ESV)

Jesus left the crowds and went into depth with His disciples (Matthew 13:36). What does "went into depth" mean? It means grounding them. Making disciples means helping them mature. It means equipping them and exhorting them to be fruitful and multiply and make more disciples. This was Jesus' last command on earth before He ascended. Let us make His final Words our first work.

Do you remember God's first command in His Word? *"Be fruitful and multiply"* (Genesis 1:28 ESV).

Practical Application Questions:

1. *"Many of His disciples turned back and no longer walked with Him"* (John 6:66 ESV). How can a person be a disciple but not a follower and worshiper of Jesus?

_____

_____

_____

_____

_____

2. What did Jesus mean the crowds came to only *"fill their bellies"* in Mark 6:26 and only *"seek after signs"* in Matthew 16:4?

_____

_____

_____

_____

_____

3. How do we come to Jesus for just Jesus, not as a means to our personal ends?

_____

_____

_____

_____

_____

Keep it simple, saint. Do not make it complicated. Do not be distracted by ministry-traditions. Be discipled. And disciple one person. Just one. And let it multiply like crazy! *"BOOM!"*

Now. What if you discipled three like Jesus did with John, James, and Peter? Imagine how much that would grow.

Year 1	3 disciple-makers of disciple-makers
Year 2	12 disciple-makers of disciple-makers
Year 3	39 disciple-makers of disciple-makers
Year 4	120 disciple-makers of disciple-makers
Year 5	363 disciple-makers of disciple-makers
Year 6	1,092 disciple-makers of disciple-makers
Year 7	3,279 disciple-makers of disciple-makers
Year 8	9,840 disciple-makers of disciple-makers
Year 9	25,523 disciple-makers of disciple-makers
Year 10	88,572 disciple-makers of disciple-makers
Year 11	265,719 disciple-makers of disciple-makers
Year 12	797,160 disciple-makers of disciple-makers
Year 13	2,391,483 disciple-makers of disciple-makers
Year 14	7,174,452 disciple-makers of disciple-makers
Year 15	21,523,359 disciple-makers of disciple-makers
Year 16	64,570,080 disciple-makers of disciple-makers

Year 17	193,710,243 disciple-makers of disciple-makers
Year 18	581,130,732 disciple-makers of disciple-makers
Year 19	**1,743,392,196 disciple-makers of disciple-makers**

Why did I stop at the 19th year? This shows that by year 19, you and just three other ordinary people from your first year will have prayerfully discipled and reached 20% of the whole world's projected population! This will have grown significantly, but the number of people groups will be relatively the same as today.

But, if we are to reach every people group and if the Gospel is to be the testimony of every people group, then the majority of that 20% by year 19 has to come from where there are the least number of disciples today. That is on the other side of the world, the hardest and darkest and poorest and least reached parts of the world.

Again, how much simpler can it be? Imagine if we get more people to be doing the same. Might we see every people group reached in our generation? Might we see disciples of every nation in 15 years? In 10 years? In 5 years?! Even sooner?

BOOM BABY!!!

Can I get a witness? Somebody shout, "*HALLELUJAH!*"

Pick a verse or seven to memorize this week to hear God's voice.
Pray these verses back to God.
Sing to Him a song of reflective worship.

SONG FOR REFLECTIVE WORSHIP
Full of Joy by M. L. Herr[39]

'Tis sweet in the presence of Jesus to dwell
Thro' troubles and trials annoy
To constantly feel His approval and smile
In this there is fullness of joy!

Fullness of joy! Yes, fullness of joy!
Serving our Master with hearts full of joy!
Soon we will finish our work here below
With fullness of joy unto Him we shall go!

Abundantly furnished with grace for our needs
When Satan attempts to decoy
Christ flies to our rescue–to victory leads
In this there is fullness of joy!

Fullness of joy! Yes, fullness of joy!
Serving our Master with hearts full of joy!
Soon we will finish our work here below
With fullness of joy unto Him we shall go!

To work for our Lord is a privilege rare
Each moment of time to employ
Co-reapers with Him in the harvest to share
In this there is fullness of joy!

Fullness of joy! Yes, fullness of joy!
Serving our Master with hearts full of joy!
Soon we will finish our work here below
With fullness of joy unto Him we shall go!

O glorious prospect- if faithful till death
Of bliss that no foe can destroy
Made one with the Bride-Groom, all nations to bless
In this there is fullness of joy!

Fullness of joy! Yes, fullness of joy!
Serving our Master with hearts full of joy!
Soon we will finish our work here below
With fullness of joy unto Him we shall go!

PRAYER JOURNAL

8. *THE OBVIOUS CONTRAST*

Commands vs. Traditions

Perhaps seeing a side-by-side contrast between what we actually read in God's Word versus the traditions of men will help.

GOD'S WORD	MAN'S TRADITION
Love God with all our heart, our soul, all our mind, all our strength. Jesus Time. Love our neighbor as we already do love ourselves. One-another one another. Gather together. Be His ambassador-witnesses. Go and make disciples. Reach the nations. Live out the Great Commandment To fulfill the Great Commission. Why? To hasten the Great Consummation! To Hasten The Wedding!	Plant a church. Build the church (which is Jesus' job). Market the church. Maintain the church. Sustain the church through: Sunday morning programs. Sunday evening programs. Wednesday evening programs. Setup-Teardown-Clean up-*Repeat*. Men's ministry. Women's ministry. Marriage ministry. Singles ministry. Single Moms' ministry. Single Dads' ministry. Divorce ministry. Counseling ministry. Children's ministry. Vacation Bible School. Youth ministry. College ministry. Senior ministry. Music ministry. Drama ministry. Coffee shop ministry. Bagel bar ministry. Hospitality ministry. Greeting ministry. Benevolence ministry. Child-care. Sunday Schools. New Members Foundations Classes. Community outreaches. Guest services. Guest follow-ups. Building cleaning. Building maintenance. Remodeling. Renovations. Upgrades. Raising funds. Distributing funds. Administrative functions. Meetings. Meetings. And more meetings! Paying the bills—mortgage or rent, utilities, supplies, upkeep and replacements, salaries, etc. Then there is all the "needed" advertising for the church. Marketing. Merchandising. Branding. Photography. Website. Social media. Meetings. Meetings. And more meetings! And on and on and on and on and on…

Simple vs. Complicated

The simple commands from God's Word versus the complicated ministry-traditions of men. Which is more feasible? Which is simple? Which is not burdensome?

As Robbi and I have begun to downsize to get ready for the Philippines, we look at everything we have accumulated, remind ourselves, *"you don't need what you don't need,"* and ask, *"will we be needing this in the Philippines?"* She has also started to watch and enjoy shows on minimalism.

Take a quick look again at the two columns on the previous page. The 1st would be minimalism. The other column? People who hoard. Have you ever seen an episode? I have not been able to finish the one episode I started. It was claustrophobic and suffocating just watching it, much less living in it. But I understand it. I felt the same way when all the "necessary" ministry-traditions were choking my life. Remember the page without margins? My son, Runner, looked at that today and the emotion he said he felt was *"overwhelming."*

Consider the Cost

"Ponder the path of your feet; then all your ways will be sure" (Proverbs 4:26 ESV).

"Now great crowds accompanied Him, and He turned and said to them, 'If anyone comes to Me and does not hate his own father and mother and wife and children and brothers and sisters, yes, and even his own life, he cannot be My disciple. Whoever does not bear his own cross and come after Me cannot be My disciple. For which of you, desiring to build a tower, does not first sit down and count the cost, whether he has enough to complete it? Otherwise, when he has laid a foundation and is not able to finish, all who see it begin to mock him, saying, 'This man began to build and was not able to finish'" (Luke 14:26-30 ESV).

Ponder the path of your feet and consider the cost. How simple is this? How complicated is this? How much will this cost in currency? How much will this cost my mental, emotional, and physical reserves? How much will this cost my marriage? My family? What is the cost of loving God and loving our neighbor? Of one-anothering one another? Of making disciples?

Being available. Opening your home. Transparency and living by example. And with simple gatherings, 100% of tithes and giving can go toward missions and help the poor and suffering.

At our simple little home church on E Street, 100% of tithes and gifts go toward missions, and to help the poor and suffering. Not one penny pays me because I am not a professional pastor, and besides, I already have a salary. Not one cent goes toward the utilities, mortgage, furniture, or maintenance for a building because we meet in our house, which is already furnished and maintained. Nothing is spent on competitive advertising because we are not trying to attract other Christians away from their fellowships. Nothing is spent on food for our gatherings because everybody brings what they have to share. Everything is given completely for the mission of reaching the unchurched, unloved, and unreached.

Do you know how your tithe is being spent? While most churches create financial reports, the majority of them do not share them with the congregation. Do you know how much is being spent to make your building more appealing? How much is spent on interest on loans? On programs to coddle and entertain the already-reached? How much, if any, is actually going to the hardest, darkest, and poorest places on the other side of the world where most of the unreached and suffering are?

According to Andrew Scott, the president of Operation Mobilization, *"Americans have spent more money buying Halloween costumes for their pets than the amount given to reach the unreached."*[40] [40]MORE IS SPENT ON PETS!!! Are you kidding me?!?!

With the traditional church model, only 5% is spent on reaching the lost. ONLY 5%?!?!?!?! The rest of it is spent on salaries, mortgages or rents, utilities, marketing, programs, programs, programs, etc. ETC!!! You know what is crazy? That 95% is spent to "reach" the already reached! For what? Check this link: <u>How Churches Spend their Money | Pacific Northwest UMC News Blog (pnwumc.org)</u>.[41]

I know of a church that spent $5,000 for the women's restroom, not because it was not functional, but for a remodel. That is not a lot, really, but when the man who pastors suggested a measly bake sale for the 5 people leaving for missions to the other side of the world, then $5,000 was very luxurious and over the top. Another church held a $40,000 fundraiser for a parking lot, even though they already had a completely functional parking lot. They just wanted a nicer one. Someone recently shared with me that one denomination spent millions just on the interest on their loans last year! Millions! Not on anything tangible, but on interest. The ironic thing is that most of these churches probably teach their members *Financial Peace* by Dave Ramsey,[42] who teaches to avoid paying interest.

In *Letters to the Church*, Francis Chan describes how when fellowships grow, they "need" a bigger venue.[43] They grow some more and "need" even bigger venues. Therefore, borrowing and spending millions on interest—for a building! And because they have now bound themselves and the congregation as *"slaves of the lender"* (Proverbs 22:7 ESV), they must keep people coming and coming, and of course, giving to pay for these ridiculous loans.

Friends, millions and millions are being spent on **unnecessary** things! We must stop and consider the cost of following man's traditions. And this is just the financial cost. The Burnout Statistics from Chapter 2 show the cost of emotional and physical health, the cost of relationships, and the cost of wasted time.

What is The Fruit?

Doing all and only what God commands, simple discipleship should produce grounded, mature, equipped, and fruitful disciple-makers of disciple-makers every year and multiplying each year after.

Following the ministry-traditions the Church has been tirefully employing for so long, we would be lucky if the men who pastor last 5 years before they burn out. We might perhaps see some sporadic, temporary boosts in Church attendance, but the majority of it would be merely transfer-growth—people just transferring from one church to another.

But are they grounded? Are they mature? Are they equipped? Are they fruitful? Are they being discipled? Are they making disciples? We want to be sure of this because we do not want to *"run in vain or labour in vain"* (Philippians 2:16 ESV).

Look at Chapter 2 again to remind yourself of the sad statistics and testimonies of burnout, discouragement, spiritual problems, and relational breakdowns—the bad fruit of *"offering up unauthorized fire."*

Significantly More Fruit

As we saw in the last chapter, evangelizing and winning one person for Jesus everyday = 365/year X 30 years = 10,950 people. That is a whole lot of people! Woohoo! But keeping it simple, discipling just one person for a year, and reproducing means significantly more disciples.

Substantively Richer Fruit

With the primary focus of the traditional church being programs, programs, and more programs instead of Christ's command to go and make disciples, what kind of fruit are they producing? It is important to know how many disciples are being produced, but more importantly, we need to know what kind of disciples are actually being produced. The Church today is turning out a lot of passionate people but sadly their heads are pretty empty. They say they love Jesus, but they do not really know Him.

Focusing on discipling just one person for a whole year is like tutoring one student versus teaching 30 students. Everybody knows that the teacher–student ratio is seriously significant. The more students there are in a class means less time teachers have to interact and personally instruct individual students, if at all.

Simple discipleship is just the same. It is life-on-life. Just as students have a higher chance for success when he or she has more time with their teacher or tutor, same for the one you disciple. A disciple, μαθητεύσατε, is a learner, a student. So, making disciples means making more grounded, more mature, more fruitful, and more equipped believers in Jesus. Significantly more and substantively richer!

> *"Are love and joy and peace things we can actually teach in a classroom? Jesus modeled these characteristics while He walked alongside His disciples. They experienced hardship and suffering together. They experienced the power of the Spirit together. They learned love by watching Him love. True discipleship involves living life together, caring for the lost and hurting together, and experiencing victories and disappointments together"* (Until Unity by Francis Chan).[44]

Acts 2-Church OR 2021-Church

I love the Church. If we love Jesus, we ought to love what He loves. And He absolutely loves the Church. So much so that He died for His Church! The Church is His Bride! He intercedes for Her. As we learned earlier in Chapter 7, Jesus builds His Church. He sustains and sanctifies His Church. He is coming back for His Church. Woohoo and Hallelujah! Christ loves His Church. So, we too, should love His Church. It is *"through the Church, the manifold wisdom of God should be made known to the rulers and authorities in the heavenly realms"* (Ephesians 3:10 ESV).

I love the local church. So much so that since I became a worshiper of Jesus, I have not moved anywhere except for a local church. Finding and being part of a healthy biblical community for my family and I is a top priority. We relocated from New Jersey to Nebraska to be part of a church. No job and no place to live. God provided. We decided to move from Nebraska to Colorado to be part of a church. This was a bigger faith move as the cost of living in Colorado is much higher than in Nebraska. But you know what? God provided.

For most folks, the job and place to live is a higher priority than a biblically healthy community for themselves and their family. They find the college they wish to attend, or their dream job, or the place they have always wanted to live because of beaches, mountains, or both. And *then* they settle for whatever fellowship is in close proximity and a convenient drive, knowing hardly anything about the leaders or the people.

Practical Application Question:

Folks, as we mentioned in earlier chapters, your spiritual life, your soul, is of utmost importance as well as your family's. Why is finding a good church family not the top priority to find for most people?

_____

_____

_____

_____

_____

I love God's Church, and I love the local church. However, I do question and am genuinely concerned about all the traditional ways we have been "doing church."

Some of you may be wondering where the local church fits into all of what you have been reading. Well, one of the one-another commands that we are to obey is *"not neglecting to gather together"* as God's people (Hebrews 10:25 ESV).

We have heard this verse used to make people feel guilty about not "going to church," which, by the way, is not mentioned in the Bible. We are never commanded to "go to church." We do not even read that believers "went to church." We are simply to be the Church because we are the Church. We do not meet *at* the church. We meet *as* the Church. The Bible does not *suggest* that we ought to have personal contact with one another. We are *commanded* to have personal contact and engage with one another.

"The Bible doesn't support many of the popular ideas about the purpose of the church, what the meetings are to be like, or even that it should be called church If someone from today who was used to today's church worship services was transported back in time to a meeting of the ekklēsia in apostolic times, he would not recognize any relationship between the meetings of the ekklēsia and the meetings of today's church. Why? Because there is none" (Peter Ditzel).[45]

"Imagine yourself stranded on a deserted island with nothing but a copy of the Bible. You have no experience with Christianity whatsoever, and all you know about the Church will come from your reading of the Bible. How would you imagine a church to function? Seriously? Close your eyes for two minutes and try to picture church as you would know it. Now think of your current church experience. Is it even close?" (Francis Chan)[46]

Is it even close? When we read and see in Scripture how God's Church looked versus our current experiences with church, is it even close? If we are able to hop in the DeLorean-Time-Machine with Marty McFly and travel back to the first century instead of November 5, 1955, would we see any similarities between Acts 2-Church and church today? No. Why? Because there are so few.

Yes, we are commanded to meet together. But what does *"meet together"* mean? The Greek is ἐπισυναγωγὴν (pronounced *ep-ee-soon-ag-o-Gay'*), and the simplest meaning is obvious, and that is simply, meet together and gather together.

There is order, not confusion in the gathering, but the Bible does not suggest that it is an "event" or "production," as we typically see, experience, and volunteer to help put together and tear down on Sunday mornings.

Robbi and I love truly hosting people in our home. As I mentioned earlier, we tell folks all the time, *"Our house is open 25 hours per day!"* And we truly mean it. If you are in our area, please come on over.

An oft-repeated conversation we have is:

Me: *Potluck, Baby! Woohoo!*
Robbi: *Great! Who's coming?*
Me: *Oh, everybody! And anybody who's nobody!*
Robbi: *OK. What's the plan?*
Me: *Let's just keep it simple.*
Robbi: *Simple, huh? Hmm...*
Me: *We grill whatever we have and whatever others bring.*
Robbi: *But what if nobody brings anything?*
Me: *Well, I guess we just share what we have.*
Robbi: *It may not be enough.*
Me: *No worries. It will be easy.*
Robbi: *It is never that easy.*
Me: *Well, we do not have to get carried away and make it a big production.*
Robbi: *Still...*
Me: *Still what?*
Robbi: *Still never that easy.*
Me: *Yethh well...*

And she is right. Fellas, our wives are always right. Most of the time. Kinda. She is almost always probably right. Actually, marriage is a relationship in which one is always right and the other is the husband.

In truth, we are both right!
1. We do not have to get carried away.
2. We do not have to make it a big production.
3. It is never that easy to meet with other people.

Who knows what people will bring or if they will bring anything? Who knows if people will come early or stick around to help clean up? Who knows if people will help grill or cook or set up the table, or if we even have a table set up? Some or all of this may take place. The simple point is this—be together.

The day of rest should be a day of rest. It is commanded by God to be a day of rest, but way too many of our Sundays have been consumed with the hustling and bustling, and busyness with *"unauthorized fires"* for a meeting that lasts maybe one hour? Two hours? And then we hustle and bustle again to put it all away. Is this really what God intended for the Sabbath? This is what Sundays have become for too many folks—they go because they feel guilty if they do not. Sadly, that hour or two is the extent of their Christian life.

"There are those who are interested in going to church for a one-hour service but have no desire to enter into deep relationships" (Francis Chan).[47]

The point of Hebrews 10:25 is simple and does not need to be so complicated. We do not neglect to meet together. We are commanded to be gathering together, to be meeting together. What does that mean? We have a gathering. We simply gather together with one another.

Though it is not always easy to get together, we have a gathering and remember that it does not need to be a big production. While it does not need to be a big event, there still must be order in our gathering. Yes, regularly meet together and spontaneously get together, but spontaneity does not mean confusion, disorder, or chaos.

We do not need to put together an event. Jesus and His disciples did not. Obviously, as they did not plan ahead to have the food to feed the crowds that gathered. With the biblically broader context of the one-anothers, our meeting together should not be limited to only one scheduled hour or two for one day a week. The one-anothers are about doing everyday life together.

Can Acts 2:42 be any clearer and simpler? *"They devoted themselves to the apostles' teaching and the fellowship, to the breaking of bread and the prayers"* (ESV).

Let us look at the side-by-side contrast chart again between Acts 2-Church with man's traditions of church:

ACTS 2-CHURCH	2021-CHURCH
Gathering together Worshiping God Preaching God's Word (2 Timothy 4:2) Devoting to the God's Word–Equipping the Saints (ETS) from the men who are elders Loving our neighbor as we love ourselves. One-anothering one another. Fellowshipping together Eating together Praying with and for one another "Hospitaliting" (as in showing hospitality to one another and even strangers) Being God's ambassador-witnesses Making disciples Reaching the nations **Hastening The Wedding!**	Plant a church. Build the church (which is Jesus' job!). Market the church. Maintain the church. Sustain the church through: Sunday morning programs. Sunday evening programs. Wednesday evening programs. Setup-Teardown-Clean up-*Repeat*. Men's ministry. Women's ministry. Marriage ministry. Singles ministry. Single Moms' ministry. Single Dads' ministry. Divorce ministry. Counseling ministry. Children's ministry. Vacation Bible School. Youth ministry. College ministry. Senior ministry. Music ministry. Drama ministry. Coffee shop ministry. Bagel bar ministry. Hospitality ministry. Greeting ministry. Benevolence ministry. Child-care. Sunday Schools. New Members Foundations Classes. Community outreaches. Guest services. Guest follow-ups. Building cleaning. Building maintenance. Remodeling. Renovations. Upgrades. Raising funds. Distributing funds. Administrative functions. Meetings. Meetings. And more meetings! Paying the bills—mortgage or rent, utilities, supplies, upkeep and replacements, salaries, etc. Then there is all the "needed" advertising for the church. Marketing. Merchandising. Branding. Photography. Website. Social media. Meetings. Meetings. And more meetings!

Does Acts 2-Church look like today's church in the other column? *"Is it even close?"* The closest examples I can think of is what God did during the late 60s and 70s with the Jesus Movement and Calvary Chapel House Churches and what He has been doing with "We Are Church" in the Bay Area. I am most excited about what God is currently doing with Spirit & Truth House Churches in northern Colorado, where my most favored son-in-law, Micah, is pastoring with his best friend, Rob.

What did 2020 teach us about church? Many people felt lost without being able to meet in their building. It was so troubling to hear Christians complain and demand their rights for their churches to be open. First of all, as Christians, we have died to all our rights. We have no more rights as we no longer live for ourselves (Galatians 2:20). Second of all, it became clearly obvious after a while that these folks were not demanding for their churches to be open but that their buildings be open.

One of the biggest things the government-controlled and imposed shutdowns showed us is that though all of us will *say* that the Church is God's people, it was apparent that most people actively believed that their church is the building. Once their buildings shut down, so did the life of their church. When the buildings were shut down, people complained about what they could *not* do—meet in their buildings. They totally forgot or ignored ALL they *could* do—still being the Church! Still loving one another. Still serving one another. Still meeting together in their homes. Still one-anothering one another.

When Zoom meetings began, we thought, *"OK. Nothing really wrong with that. A quick band-aid."* But it did not go beyond that. You cannot adequately care for and shepherd people and be an example to the flock (1 Peter 5:3) through a computer screen or a pre-recorded multi-edited YouTube sermon.

So, we prepared food. Together with a bottle of sparkling juice and a tiny packet of salt, we delivered meals and boxes of food to families to bless them by showing God's love in a tangible way. We fellowshipped with them and prayed for them at their front doors, face to face, looked into their eyes, and encouraged them in the Lord. We showed that although the buildings may be shut down, God's Church did not! Hallelujah!

Throughout the country, believers began to gather in parks, beaches, bridges, backyards, driveways, and living rooms to pray and worship. Buildings were closed. Traditional churches shut down all their meetings. God's Church did not!

Our home is a gathering place for people to come and eat and talk and laugh and cry and pray and play and read good books and worship and be equipped from God's Word. Goodness, people even come over when we are not here! We came home one day and found one of our college students sleeping soundly on our living room floor. We also bring people in need of a home into our home: meth and heroin addicts, aimless college students, struggling single moms, and troubled teens, caring for them, discipling them, and sending them out into the world, prayerfully to make more disciples of Jesus.

The Doctrine of Crashing and Community

Our friends, Bruce and Natalie Sivil, taught us what they called the "Doctrine of Crashing." Because, well, they loved to crash our house! And we loved when they did. We have shared this with everybody we know — that our house is open 25 hours per day, and you can crash us anytime! Is this not what God's Church is supposed to look like? Community? Real genuine community where "*all who believed were together*" in community (Acts 2:44 ESV). This is God's Church vs. today's traditional church of 2021. "*Is it even close?*"

There is a Facebook Page called Connecting Christian Roommates in Denver. I am so confused when I see people stating, "*I am plugged into my church*" or "*I really love my church*," but "*still looking for community*." Plugged in but still needing community? Does that make any sense? Again, Acts 2-Church vs. traditional 2021 church —is it even close?

When we say community, we do not mean getting together for a ministry planning meeting. When was the last time you were invited to a leader's house for just a meal? A game? A movie? Just to hang out and get to know each other? Or invited by a leader for lunch after Sunday church? We always try to invite new people every Sunday either to our home or a restaurant to bless them with lunch and to be blessed by hearing their stories.

We have been invited to hundreds of meetings, but Robbi and I cannot recall ever being invited to a leader's home for a meal that was not also a meeting. I did go to a leader's home once to watch UFC, but it does not really count, as I invited myself when I heard he was going to be watching it.

Perhaps Acts 2-Church was able to experience genuine community because they were not completely exhausted like 2021 churches because of all the "necessary" ministry-traditions.

So, let us not neglect "*to meet together*" (Hebrews 10:25 ESV), not *at* the church, but *as* the church. Let us worship God together; preach and teach God's Word; devote ourselves to God's Word; equip the saints (ETS); love our neighbor as we love ourselves, one-another one another; fellowship together; eat together; pray with and for one another; show hospitality to one another; be God's ambassador-witnesses; make disciples; reach the nations; and hasten The Wedding!

Practical Application Questions:

1. What jumps out the most in the obvious contrasts?

_____

_____

_____

_____

_____

2. On a 1-10 scale of 1 being Acts 2-Church and 10 being traditional 2021-Church, where do you see most churches? Your church?

_____

_____

_____

_____

_____

3. How much of your giving is going to pay for salaries, buildings, interest on loans, etc? How much is actually going to reach the lost and the poor among the unreached, not the already reached?

_____

_____

_____

_____

_____

4. How and where do you see genuine community happening?

_____

_____

_____

_____

_____

5. What do think of opening your home and "hospitaliting"? What are some fears or excuses? How can it be exciting?

_____

_____

_____

_____

_____

Pick a verse or eight from this chapter to memorize this week to hear God's voice.

Pray these verses back to God.

Sing to Him a song of reflective worship.

SONG FOR REFLECTIVE WORSHIP
Bring Me Back to My First Love [48]

Bring me back to my first love
Help me remember from where I've fallen'
Bring to me the sweet memories
Of the fire that once burned bright as the sun
Bring me back to where I belong
Bring me back to my first love

Bring me back and cleanse my heart
And renew a willing spirit again
Please don't turn away
Lord, help me learn today
Let me burn, I pray with holy fire within
Restore the joy of Your salvation
Bring me back to You

Speak Your wisdom in my inmost being
Lord I want to know and hear Your voice
And in Your lovingkindness
Make me hear Your joy and gladness
Let my brokenness rejoice. Rejoice!

Bring me back to my first love
Help me do the things I used to do
But not to do, Lord, just to do
But because I am Your child all through
Bring me back
Bring me back to my first love
Bring me back to You

PRAYER JOURNAL

9. *SO,* WHY *SIMPLE DISCIPLESHIP?*

This is what excites me most because the "fruit" of Simple Discipleship is the ultimate end and answer to *Why Simple Discipleship*!

Passive or Active

Unless you are a sad preterist, most of us would agree that we are still waiting for and anticipating the triumphant return of our Lord Jesus Christ. Much of what is preached regarding Christ's return is about waiting and being prepared for it, which is not unbiblical. It is taught in Scripture to be ready as it was taught in the early Church.

> *"It would appear that the early Christians believed that Christ might come at any time, even in their days; the first advent, being so recent, excited within them the expectation of the immediateness of the second. Hence the doctrine of the second advent occupied a much more prominent place in the thoughts of the primitive Christians than it does in ours. It was to them a living power; believers then lived in constant expectation of the coming of the Lord..."* (The Pulpit Commentary — 1 Thessalonians).[49]

But how is the Church today regarding the return of Jesus? When was the last time you heard preaching or teaching about His return? Is the doctrine of the second advent a prominent place in the pulpit or our thoughts? When was the last time you heard the topic of Christ's return in casual conversation with another Christian brother or sister?

We had the privilege of homeschooling our kids and sending them to private school when they got older. One of the ways I challenged them was to not just wait for a teacher to bring up Jesus. That was to be expected. I asked them if anyone initiated conversations about Jesus outside of class, not in the context of a lesson or homework, but while talking about seeing a new movie, the latest TikTok, or mentioning your time with a good friend.

We are so inclined to talk about a lot of things, but when was the last time you just brought up Jesus? When was the last time you brought up the subject of His return?

Waiting for and being ready for Jesus' return is biblical, but it is incomplete, short-sighted, and much of the fruit is luke-warm Christianity and mediocrity, an encouragement to sloth and security.

"...whereas the teaching of the present day has in a measure passed from it. Its uncertainty, instead of exciting us to holiness and watchfulness, is too often abused as an encouragement to sloth and security" (The Pulpit Commentary—1 Thessalonians).[50]

As we have been saying throughout this book we go and make disciples not because it is a tradition passed down to us, but because Jesus commands us. But we cannot just *passively wait* for His return. We go and make disciples for the purpose of **actively hastening** Christ's return. Hastening the return of Jesus is *why* we go and make disciples! His return is our motive for Why Simple Discipleship. Are you just passively waiting, or are you actively hastening?

Beginning with the End in Mind

The Great Consummation. The Joy of all joys! There is no greater motivation. What motivates you?

I've spoken with many young, engaged men and women. *"So, you're engaged. That's awesome! I love marriage! Marriage and all it brings is a gift to be received aggressively with wholehearted thanksgiving and passion. So, when's the wedding?"* Many times, I am surprised when a lot of them say they have no date yet or are going to wait a few more years. They have been engaged for a while already, but they are going to wait? And I am like, *"Umm. Why? You do not want to get married?"*

There is an old evangelism method that is still quite effective today. There are multiple variations of it, which is good. It needs to be personalized and fit the particular occasion and the person or persons being addressed. I am not referring to changing the Gospel in any way.

This evangelism method is called the ATW, which stands for "*And Then What?*"

You meet a young person who just graduated high school and ask them, "*And then what?*"
And they answer, "*oh, probably get into university.*"
And then you ask, "*ATW?*"
And they say, "*oh, get a good job,*"
And you ask, "*ATW?*"
And they reply, "*If I'm lucky, probably get married.*"
And you ask again, "*ATW?*"
And they respond, "*Buy a house, have kids, raise a family.*"

Now you may want to change it up a bit here or talk about family and kids, work, hobbies, or safe subjects like politics or covid and government censorship. Otherwise, they may find you really annoying like a little kid always asking, "*ATW? ATW? ATW?... Why? Why? Why?*"

But eventually, you get to ask, "*And so, after kids, what then?*"

See how I masterfully disguise my question there? They will most likely say, "*Retire. Enjoy old age and grandbabies.*" And you talk about retirement. Talk about grandbabies, because they are very special, especially mine! "*Where do you want to retire? What will you do?*"

But is that the end? Can we ask ATW again? Of course, you can. And you must! "*Uhm so, ATW after retirement?*" And if they are not already irritated with you and ready to punch you or walk away just yet, like Abraham, you ask again, ... "*Soooo... then what?*" And they say, "*Then what!? Then what?! Then I guess I die.*"

Can we ask even one more time? Oh, heavens yes! Please ask because as Christians who read and know our Bibles, we know there is a "then what" after we die! So, in a spirit of "*gentleness and respect*" as we are instructed in 1 Peter 3:16, we ask, "*I mean this in all seriousness and sincerity, what then after you die?*"

There are many answers people will give you, but my point is this: the answer to this last and final question should determine the answers for all the preceding questions. The goal answered in this question is the most important. Begin with the end in mind. The problem is people do not think about it and do not wish to.

Destination Gives Us Direction

I love this line from another tv series, *"Destination gives us direction."* Destination gives us direction! Yes! The end determines our steps, our plans, and our goals.

I ask my employees regularly, *"What do you want to earn this year? Because if you want to earn this much this year, you need to earn this much every month, which means you need to earn this much every week, which means you need to earn this much every day, which means you must do these specific things every day! The goal of the year determines what you do each month, what you do each week, and what you do every day."* Begin with the end in mind. Why? Because destination gives us direction for every step.

What is the goal of your life? What is your end? The goal of your life—of after life—needs to determine what you do every day. ATW is the big WHY YOU DO WHAT YOU DO EVERY DAY!

One of my favorite authors, Jonathan Edwards, wrote one of my favorite books, *The End For Which God Created The World*. [51]Basically, why did God create the world; what was His goal of creating it. And Edwards spends a good chunk of the book defining the word "end" and distinguishing between subordinate ends, chief ends, final ends, and ultimate ends. What is the end of life? After death, and then what? Is there a greater end? What is the chief end of your life? What is the ultimate end? Because that final end should determine why you do what you do with your life, year, month, week, day, job, family, marriage, everything.

With everything we do, we can always ask, *"To what end?"* or, *"And then what?"* because everything always has a greater end. 99% of everything is always a subordinate end to another end. We work—to what end? To earn a paycheck. Is that it? Do we get our paycheck and just hold it and stare at it? Is that the end? No, we earn it for another end. To buy a meal. To save for a house. But still, you go on and ask why? To what end do we buy a meal or a house? Just to stare at the meal? Just to own a piece of property? Why do we do what we do? What is our ultimate end? What is the final end? What is *our* final end? What is man's final end? Is it death? Do we just eat and drink and take one last breath and die? Is that our end?

As Christians, we know that is not our end. We know that man's end is either in hell or heaven. But is just being in heaven our end? Yes, the wonders of heaven will be beyond our wildest imaginations. But will we not tire eventually of looking at streets of gold?

By our nature, we grow weary of things. That is why children want a new toy the very next day. We love something initially, and eventually, we take it for granted. The honeymoon period does not last forever. Even golden streets may begin to fade in our eyes. That is the inevitability of all things created. As creatures, we will eventually lose our fascination with the created. We take all things and sadly, people for granted.

Everything and everyone has been created. All of our toys and treasures have expiration dates. What about what is not created? What about *Who* is not created? There is only One. He alone holds this title. He was not created. God Himself is The Creator.

"For by Him all things were created, in heaven and on earth, visible and invisible, whether thrones or dominions or rulers or authorities—all things were created through Him and for Him" (Colossians 1:16 ESV).

There is so much we can still study and learn about our spouses. *"What gives her goosebumps? What makes him shudder? Why do her eyes light up when she sees a particular person or when she hears a certain thing? What memories bring a tear to his eyes? Why does she love sleep and shiplap so much? What is his love affair with guns and gaming? How long has she felt this way about clothes and eating habits? How often does he meditate on work, on sports, on me?* We can go on and on, yes? It will take a lifetime. And that is the point.

Now... imagine God. How long before we exhaust His beauty? How long before we can finally learn everything there is to know about God? How long before we lose our wonder and amazement of our Savior? On this side of eternity, while still in our flesh which grows weary and we take gifts for granted, we lose our wonder, even of God. But on the other side of eternity, when sin can no longer tempt us because we are no longer in our flesh, how long can we gaze upon the glory and beauty and majesty of God?

"Could we with ink the ocean fill
And were the skies of parchment made
Were every stalk on earth a quill
And every man a scribe by trade
To write the love of God above
Would drain the oceans dry
Nor could the scroll contain the whole
Though stretched from sky to sky"
(The Love of God by Frederick Martin Lehman 1917)[52]

"When we've been there ten thousand years
Bright shining as the sun
We've no less days to sing God's praise
Than when we first begun!"
(Amazing Grace by John Newton)[53]

After ten thousand years, or more accurately even after a trillion times a trillion eternities, we will be singing as if we had just begun to sing! Why? Because we will never exhaust God's mystery and majesty and beauty and greatness and glory! The Bible tells us His glory is everlasting to everlasting.

"From everlasting to everlasting, You are God" (Psalm 90:2 ESV).

"Great is the Lord and greatly to be praised, and His greatness is unsearchable" (Psalm 145:3 ESV).

"And the four living creatures, each of them with six wings, are full of eyes all around and within, and day and night, they

never cease to say, "Holy, holy, holy is the Lord God Almighty, Who was and is and is to come" (Revelations 4:8 ESV).

This means there is no end to God. No end to knowing Him. No end in discovering more of Him. No end to gazing at His beauty, for His beauty never fades.

All Seek Happiness

Back to our question, *"Why simple discipleship?"* In determining why we do all we do, there is another component we need to acknowledge.

Frenchman Blaise Pascal wrote in the *Pensées*[54] said that every man strives for happiness, either by going to battle or even ending his own life. Tolstoy writes in *Family Happiness*[55] that he found what is needed for happiness: quiet country isolation, nature, some rest, good books, useful employment, music, love for our neighbor, a mate, kids. Then he asks, *"what more can a man desire?"* What more? Come on, Christian. You know this answer, or you ought to know. What more? Can these things bring eternal and everlasting happiness? No! They are broken cisterns, all!

Also in *The End For Which God Created The World*, Jonathan Edwards writes that the soul that acknowledges the majesty of God does not glorify God as much as the soul that acknowledges God's majesty *and* delights in God's majesty.[56] He not only acknowledges God, but also enjoys God. Knowing God with our minds and enjoying God with our hearts. To know intimately and to be intimately known.

See, the devil and his demons know Who God is. They even know that Jesus is God. But they do not enjoy that Jesus is God. They do not find Him beautiful. They do not find Him wonderful. They do not find Him amazing.

According to almost every sermon from John Piper, and every one of his books, we glorify God most *BY* enjoying Him forever. Do we glorify God by serving Him? Yes. By doing our duty? Yes. But, not as much as the man that serves from his delight in God. We glorify God most by enjoying *Him*. Finding our joy and satisfaction and fulfillment and happiness and treasure in *Him*.

Since there is no end to understanding God, learning about Him, gazing upon His beauty, and since our happiness in Him can never be exhausted, what does that mean?

Do you know Jesus today? Yes? Hallelujah and Woohoo! That is wonderful. That is fantastic. That is amazing! Is knowing Jesus here on earth the happiest you could ever be? Let me ask this way, *"Is that the end? Is this day the happiest you could ever be? Can we still ask, 'And Then What?'"*

We hop on a plane in Denver. Why? What is our destination? The Philippines? Pakistan? The 10/40 window? Why? To reach unreached peoples. Why? To make disciples. Why? And then what? They are discipled. And then what?

Everything is temporal. Everything is *temporal*. In John 17:3, the Bible tells us that only One is eternal and knowing Him is eternal life. Knowing God and knowing Him intimately for eternity is the final and ultimate end of all ends. There is nothing greater. There is no further end to that.

Remember the young couple I mentioned at the beginning of this chapter who were in no rush to have a wedding date? They were going to wait several more years. Really? Why in the world would you want to wait to finally be with the love of your life?

When Robbi and I were engaged, I was the happiest I could ever be AND the most miserable! Do you know why? Because I always had to say goodnight and leave! I was happy and at the same time, not! The wedding could not come soon enough.

Before their wedding, the two people are a giddy and happy engaged couple; always laughing, smiling, and being disgustingly cute. But how long would that have lasted after a few years or twenty years of engagement and still no wedding? How long before one of them asks, *"Do you really love me? Don't you want to get married?"* How long before one eventually asks, *"After this year, and then what?"*

This is the sad state of the Church today: apathetic about remaining engaged for two thousand years, not even thinking about the return of Jesus, or longing for the Wedding in the least.

Hasten the Day!

> *"But the day of the Lord will come like a thief, and then the heavens will pass away with a roar, and the heavenly bodies will be burned up and dissolved, and the earth and the works that are done on it will be exposed. Since all things are thus to be dissolved, what sort of people ought you to be in lives of holiness and godliness, waiting for and **hastening** the coming of the day of God."* (2 Peter 3:10 ESV)

Wait! What? Did we read that correctly? Hastening the day of God? When I first read that, I remember it jumped out of the page and slapped me upside the head! *"We can hasten the return of Jesus? We can get Jesus here sooner? I can hasten The Wedding? This is amazing! I do not need to wait until I die? What do I need to do?"*

I had help from Matthew 24, which tells us about 7 things that need to happen before Jesus returns. But ONLY ONE is on us. There is something we as the Church can do and must do.

Matthew 24:14 (ESV) says, *"this Gospel of the Kingdom will be proclaimed throughout the whole world as a testimony to…"* every person? No. Every people group, *"and **then** the end."* The Gospel will be preached to every people group as a testimony, meaning this will be the testimony of every people group, that they are reached for Christ. It *will* happen. It will *happen*! It is a promise.

And then what? The end. What is the end?

THE JOY OF ALL JOYS!

The Wedding. The JOY of all joys! The Great Consummation! *This* is the ultimate then-what! A blissful eternity of knowing God. We can hasten the day (2 Peter 3:12) by making disciples and reaching every unreached people group!

George Ladd helped me greatly with his little book, *The Gospel of The Kingdom.*[57] He says we do not only have the privilege of waiting but of hastening that end! If our greatest happiness is The Great Consummation, if our greatest happiness is the marriage supper of the Lamb with His Bride, then will we not bend every effort toward that end? Will we not do everything to reach every Unreached People Group for that end and toward that glorious and beautiful end? For *"my desire is to be with Christ, for that is far better"* (Philippians 1:23 ESV). Is it far better for you?

Why reach every people group and make disciples of every nation? Just to see revival in the world and nothing more? So that every people group is reached and nothing more? No "then what" after that?! Why do I do all I do? To hasten The Wedding. Why should we do all we do? To hasten The Wedding. Why do all and only what God commands? To hasten The Wedding. Why reach the nations? To hasten The Wedding! **Why Simple Discipleship? To hasten the Wedding. To hasten the Wedding. To hasten the Wedding!** God is our end. There is no greater end after this. He and The Wedding is the final "then what."

We, His Church, are the Bride. Jesus is our Bridegroom, and right before the Wedding, our Bridegroom left. If the Bride truly loves Him, she cannot be happy with the status quo. She cannot act as if nothing is wrong. And IF she loves Him, IF she is longing for The Wedding, His Church will do whatever it takes to reach every unreached people group. *IF* she loves Him...

Steps to Hasten the Wedding:
7. The Wedding
6. The Return of Jesus
5. Longing for The Wedding with Jesus
4. Longing for Jesus to return
3. Loving Jesus
2. Knowing Jesus
1. Seeing Jesus

If we want The Wedding, we need to first help people see Jesus. Before people bend every effort to hasten The Wedding, they need to first long for The Wedding. Before they long for The Wedding, they need to first long for Jesus to return. Before they long for Jesus to return, they need to be in love with Jesus. Before they love Him, they need to know Him. Before they know

Him, they need to see Him. If we want The Wedding, we need to first help people see Jesus. Once they see Jesus for Who He really is as portrayed in His Word and the more they see Him, they will get to know Him. The more they get to know Him from His Word and communion—Jesus Time—the more they will love Him. The more they love Him, the more they will long for His return. The more they long for His return, the more they will long for The Wedding. Therefore, we must turn their eyes upon Jesus. Hence the vital importance and non-negotiability of Jesus Time. We must model and teach people to spend intimate time with Jesus. Everything flows from here. I cannot stress this enough.

Jesus' disciples changed the world because they spent time with Him.

The command to make disciples is a command, not a suggestion. It is more than a good idea to pass the time away. It is not just another thing to try to squeeze into your schedule that is already full of ministry-traditions. This IS our ministry. As Francis Chan said, "*It is the mission of our lives.*" Again, ministry-traditions are good, but they were never commanded by Jesus. Go and make disciples is His command to us. This is our ministry. This is our mission.

Aside from obeying it because it is His command, aside from being the way Jesus did it, aside from doing it because it is easy and not burdensome, we have a greater and higher motivation, the greatest and highest motivation—the quick return of Jesus! What could be a greater or higher motivation than that? That is IF you really love Jesus and want to see Him return...

Let me ask you again: maybe you do think of His return, but are you just passively waiting for it? Or are you doing whatever you can to actively hasten His return because you know that nothing will make you happier than to see Him face to face?

Listen. A generation in the Bible is 40 years. Jesus said, *"the Gospel will reach every people group and then the end,"* (Matthew 24:14 ESV). He also said it will be that same generation who will see His return, *"Truly, I say to you, that generation* (who sees all those things happen) *will not pass away until all these things take place,"* (Matthew 24:34 ESV).

> *"Here is the motive of our mission: the final victory awaits the completion of our task. 'And then the end will come.' There is no other verse in the Word of God which says, 'And then the end will come.'*
> *When is Christ coming again? When the Church has finished its task. When will This Age end? When the world has been evangelized.*
> *'What will be the sign of Your coming and of the close of the age?' (Matt. 24:3). 'This gospel of the kingdom will be preached throughout the whole world as a testimony to all nations; and then, AND THEN, the end will come.'*
> *When? Then, when the Church has fulfilled its divinely appointed mission. Do you love the Lord's appearing? Then* **you will bend every effort to take the Gospel into all the world.** *It troubles me in the light of the clear teaching of God's Word, in the light of our Lord's explicit definition of our task in The Great Commission, that we take it so lightly. 'All authority in heaven and on earth has been given to Me.' This is the Good News of the Kingdom....*
> *His is the kingdom; He reigns in heaven, and He manifests His reign on earth in and through His church. When we have accomplished our mission, He will return and establish His kingdom in glory.*
> *To us it is given not only to wait for but also to hasten the coming of the day of God. This is the mission of the Gospel of the Kingdom, and this is our mission"* (George E. Ladd).[58]

What does this mean? I am glad you asked. It means that Jesus will *not* return until the Gospel reaches every people group. Therefore, IF you really love Jesus, if HE is truly your highest joy

147

and satisfaction and fulfillment and happiness and treasure, then you will *"bend every effort to take the Gospel into all the world."*

Spending or Sending?

But will this happen if we spend most of our resources here on "unnecessary" things? Remember from Chapter 8: 95% of the Church's money is spent on itself in areas where there are already many existing churches and have been for years, even decades! Only 5% is spent on reaching the lost. How much is actually sent to the unreached areas of the world, where there are no disciples to reach their own people?

Where is most of our *personal* money being spent? On ourselves. We also saw that we spend more money on Halloween costumes for pets than for reaching the lost. Pets over people?!

Growing up in the States is a very comfortable life for the most part. The majority of people here have more than enough and more than they need. Many things which most of the world goes without have become "necessary" here, such as air-conditioning, your own room, a second car, two refrigerators, an extra freezer, cable tv, a second living room, a private master bathroom, a manicured lawn, even health insurance or life insurance... The list can go on and on and on of what billions of people go without. Do we even see how lavishly we spend on clothing, on food of which we waste so much, entertainment, our toys, and then our bigger and bigger homes that we now "need" to store them all? Perhaps this is the reason why so many of us do not go when God clearly says, *"Go"* (Matthew 28:19). We have made ourselves too comfortable, or worse—we have become dependent on all our comforts.

We have been abundantly blessed, but we have been blessed to be a blessing, to help, not to hoard. We should be sending the majority of our resources where the need is greatest—to the hardest and darkest places among the unreached peoples of the world—not to the already reached.

If we follow God's simple command to go and make disciples, focus and pour into just one disciple a year and multiply that year after year after year, do you think every people group will be reached? Can we imagine it not happening?!

What does this mean? It means that by letting Jesus do *HIS* job of building His Church as He said He would and by us just obeying His simple command to go and make disciple-makers of disciple-makers, we can easily see Christ Jesus return in our generation! In *our* generation! Why would we not desire that?

If It Weren't For People…

My friend, Kirk McCrimmon often says *"if it weren't for people…"* jokingly, but always in a context that hints there may be some seriousness in his joke. Discussing the idea of this book with Kirk and talking about people—not specific persons, just people in general—I believe he did say something to the effect of, *"If it weren't for people, disciple-making would be so easy."* We had a bit of a laugh because we understood that we *have* to deal with people, whom Robert Coleman says, *"were His method."* [59]We cannot *not* deal with people and people are sinners, myself being the biggest sinner I know.

"If it weren't for people, disciple-making would be so easy," because people will still be people. Just recently, one young disciple could not stop apologizing for not showing up for breakfast with me. I had to reassure him over and over again to let him know how much it was no big deal. I totally understood. You know why? Because I have done the same many times in the past to the men who were discipling me—sleeping in or completely forgetting. It was awesome how they always reassured me and showed me grace. How? Probably because they also have done the same and were shown grace by others.

"If it weren't for people, discipleship would be so easy," but sadly, there are times that the ones you disciple do not have genuine repentance but merely *"worldly grief"* over the consequences of their sin. They are more frustrated for their lack of success than their lack of love for God. *"For godly sorrow produces a repentance that leads to salvation without regret, whereas worldly grief produces death"* (2 Corinthians 7:10 ESV). They are sometimes like the ones who do not believe… *"and turned back and no longer walked with Him"* (John 6:66 ESV).

"*If it weren't for people, it would be so easy,*" because people will continue to sin. Even after you labor and pour so much of yourself into them, people will sin. Even those you take into your own home with your family will do shameful things in your house, but a life of repentance is not always perfect.

I do not know how many times I have stumbled and cried out like the Apostle Paul, "*I do not do what I want, but I do the very thing I hate* (Romans 7:15) and "*the evil I do not want is what I keep on doing!*" (Romans 7:19).

On this side of eternity, we will still fall. I know. I know it well. Mine is an imperfect repentance of stumbling, falling, getting up, crawling, getting up again, and again to run this glorious race He has set before me. Repentance does not mean never falling. But praise and thank God that though falling and stumbling and crawling is not graceful, it sure is full of His grace. Hallelujah! And thank God we can be "*sure of this, that He Who began a good work in you will bring it to completion at the day of Christ Jesus!*" (Philippians 1:6 ESV). "*For it is God Who works in you, both to will and work for His good pleasure!*" (Philippians 2:13 ESV). "*And my God will supply every need of yours*"—to run and complete this race—*according to His riches in glory in Christ Jesus!*" (Philippians 4:19 ESV).

"*If it weren't for people, making disciples would be a piece of pie,*" but thank God for His Holy Spirit! He is doing His work in all of us who are being discipled and in those we are discipling. We cannot and must not forget the Holy Spirit.

Remember The Holy Spirit

We must pause here and be reminded that Jesus said, "*apart from Me, you can do nothing*" (John 15:5 ESV). We can still sin, a lot, but apart from Him, we can do nothing good or nothing worthy (Romans 3:12). We cannot assume we can do this apart from His Holy Spirit living in us and through us. We should have the humility of Moses when he told God, "*If Your presence does not go with us, do not bring us up from here*" (Exodus 33:15 ESV) because even as simple as Jesus' plan is to go and make disciples, we cannot do this apart from Him.

As finite beings, we can only do what we can do. We are very limited in what we can do. There is quite a bit that we cannot do, such as bring the dead to life! But thank God because *He* specializes in raising the dead.

Like the Apostle Paul who begins many of his letters saying how often he prays for the saints, I too am constantly interceding for the Holy Spirit to do that which I cannot do—to open blind eyes to see the face of Christ, to open deaf ears to hear God's voice in His Word, and to soften hearts of unbelievers I am striving to reach and those who I am discipling in the faith.

When my cousin recently moved in with us earlier this year, we nor he knew what God had in store. At first, he devoured the Bible we gave him like a starving prisoner of war who was just liberated! He seemed hungry and excited for everything we poured into him, even asking for more! We pray it is sincere as he worshiped and prayed with us almost daily. He had honest hard questions, and we tried our best to answer them humbly. We directed him to the living water of God's Word to turn his eyes off of himself and toward Jesus.

This past month, we have been surviving covid together. Many times, we have shared with him that hard things (like covid) will wear us down physically, emotionally, and mentally cloud our thinking. These will either draw us closer to God to press into Him even more or reveal if our hearts are truly His. We do not know, but we pray that he is not like the seed *"on the rock… when they hear the Word, receive it with joy. But these have no root; they believe for a while, and in time of testing fall aw*ay" (Luke 8:13 ESV). Moreso, we are praying that he might be like the woman in John 4 who encountered Jesus, the Fountain of living water, when she went for a drink from the well. We believe she was filled with the living water as we are told in verse 28 that *"she left her water jar!"* She left her jar! Then she went to tell everyone about Messiah Jesus Christ! May this be true of my young cousin, whom I have grown to love as a younger brother or even a son, prayerfully, a spiritual son in the faith. Have mercy, Lord God. Holy Spirit, have Your way.

From the beginning, it has been the Holy Spirit Who regenerates and awakens a dead soul to new life. Throughout that new life, it is the same Holy Spirit Who transforms and grows the disciple of Christ. *"And I am sure of this, that He who began a good work in you will bring it to completion at the day of Jesus Christ"* (Philippians 1:6 ESV). We cannot forget the Holy Spirit, Whom Francis Chan said has become the "Forgotten God" in our country. [60]Salvation, from the very beginning to completion, is a miraculous and merciful work of God changing hearts.

> *"The world is not moved by love or actions that are of human creation. And the church is not empowered to live differently from any other gathering of people without the Holy Spirit. But when believers live in the power of the Spirit, the evidence in their lives is supernatural. The church cannot help but be different, and the world cannot help but notice"* (Francis Chan and Danae Yankoski).[61]

We cannot forget the Holy Spirit. He is not an experience, a feeling, an emotion, a strong impression, an energy, a thrill, a buzz, or a glory cloud. He is most definitely not hysteria, nor does He produce hysteria. We cannot forget the Holy Spirit because He is a Person, The third Person of the Trinity. He is The Convicter of sins, The Sealer and The Seal, The Indweller, and The Revealer of Truth. He is our Comforter, our Advocate, our Counselor, our Guide, our Intercessor, and our Teacher.

We can do this. We can make disciples. We can hasten the return of Jesus. We can see His return in our generation. But we cannot do it in our own power, for it is *"not by power, nor by might but My Spirit," says the Lord of hosts"* (Zechariah 4:6 ESV). Even after Jesus' command to go and make disciples (Matthew 28:19), He tells His disciples to wait for the Holy Spirit (Acts 1:4-5). Go, yes. But wait for the Holy Spirit.

> *"You will receive power when the Holy Spirit has come upon you, and you will be My witnesses… to the end of the earth"* (Acts 1:8 ESV).

> *"I don't want my life to be explainable without the Holy Spirit. I want people to look at my life and know that I couldn't be doing this by my own power"* (Francis Chan and Danae Yankoski).[62]

Remember God's Word

While we realize that we cannot do this apart from the Holy Spirit, neither can we do this apart from God's Word, which we pointed out and strongly encouraged in chapter 5. It is GOD's Word that has power, not ours. Sadly, too many people place more weight on "words" or "visions" or "new revelations" from people rather than God's Word where we can absolutely know for sure it IS from God. Nothing else is absolutely for sure.

I love reading biblically sound books, especially old books written by dead guys like Jonathan Edwards, Thomas Watson, Charles Spurgeon and Arthur Pink. I do like some living authors too – John Piper, Francis Chan and John MacArthur. Oh, they do not see eye to eye on every little thing, but on the main thing, well, they keep it the main thing—an all-consuming passionate concern and desire for the glory of God's Name and renown in the world (Isaiah 26:8).

See, books are wonderful. Biblically sound books, that is. I have always said to our kids that probably the greatest inheritance I will leave them is my library. Just thinking of leaving it when we go to the Philippines next year is making me anxious. I had a hard time when our realtor wanted to move some to show our house!

As I was in the early stages of writing this book, I remember my cousin was excited to be reading it. But some nights he would tell me he had to read his Bible, to which I quickly responded, *"Yes! Yes! Yes! Put everything aside. Even my book. Read your Bible!"*

As wonderful as books are, they can never ever replace the Bible. Yes, I encourage people to read good authors and I try to give away as many of the good ones as much as I can. But they are just to supplement God's Word, not substitute for It.

In conclusion, we cannot do this without drinking from the Fountain. We cannot do this without the Holy Spirit. We cannot do this apart from God's Word. We cannot do this on our own apart from God. We are totally and utterly dependent on Him.

"Walk by the Spirit and you will not gratify the desires of the flesh. For the desires of the flesh are against the Spirit, and the desires of the Spirit are against the flesh., for these are

opposed to each other, to keep you from doing the things you want to do. But if you are led by the Spirit, you are not under the law... If we live by the Spirit, let us also walk by the Spirit" (Galatians 5:16-18, 25 ESV).

"All Scripture is breathed out by God and profitable for teaching, for reproof, for correction, and for training in righteousness, that the man of God may be complete, equipped for every good work" (2 Timothy 3:16-17 ESV).

Practical Application Questions:

1. How is your desire to see Jesus? Is there any higher motivation than that? Is there any greater end than that?

_____

_____

_____

_____

_____

2. Why are you doing what you are doing? What is your end goal? What and who will make you most happy? When will you be the happiest?

_____

_____

_____

_____

_____

3. According to Matthew 24:14, what is our part and our responsibility and what do we need to be doing to hasten The Wedding?

_____

_____

_____

_____

_____

4. Things such as air conditioning and a second bathroom were luxuries just a few years ago. Now they have become "necessities." How have we, as a culture, gotten so dependent on our comforts? How have you?

_____

_____

_____

_____

_____

5. How can we get back to the basics and live more according to *"you don't need what you don't need,"* and not be so dependent on our comforts and our toys?

_____

_____

_____

_____

_____

6. How are you spending? How are you sending?

_____

_____

_____

_____

_____

7. How is the Holy Spirit *not* forgotten in your life? How is His Word central in your life?

_____

_____

_____

_____

_____

Pick a verse or seven from this chapter to memorize this week to hear God's voice.

Pray these verses back to God.

Sing to Him a song of reflective worship

SONG FOR REFLECTIVE WORSHIP
His Love is Far Better Than Gold by Alfred Henry Ackley[63]

The love of Christ is so precious
That no mortal its wealth can unfold
His grace is a storehouse of riches to me
His love is far better than gold

His love is far better than gold
Its fullness can never be told
It makes me an heir to the mansion above
For His love is far better than gold

He meets ev'ry need with the promise
No good thing from His own to withhold
So daily I trust in the Crucified One
His love is far better than gold

His love is far better than gold
Its fullness can never be told
It makes me an heir to the mansion above
For His love is far better than gold

My heart ever yearns with a longing
To behold the great joy of my soul
Forever to dwell in the presence on Him
Whose love is far better than gold

His love is far better than gold
Its fullness can never be told
It makes me an heir to the mansion above
For His love is far better than gold

PRAYER JOURNAL

_____

_____

_____

_____

_____

_____

_____

_____

_____

_____

_____

_____

_____

_____

_____

_____

_____

_____

_____

_____

_____

10. *TURN OUR EYES UPON JESUS*

Jesus of The Bible

People will not ask the big questions if Satan can just keep them distracted by the ordinary stuff of life and make them believe that is what is of real importance. I believe this is also one of the main reasons people keep themselves too busy or too entertained to think about what really matters. When we are not distracted or diverted, then we ask the big metaphysical questions: "*What is the meaning of life? Why am I here? Is there a God? What happens when we die? Is there heaven? Is there hell? Is there absolute truth?*"

The answer to these big questions can be found in the correct answer to the one huge question: Who Is Jesus?

In Mark 4, Jesus calms the storm and sea, and the disciples ask, "*Who is this Guy that the wind and sea obey Him?*" Jesus Himself asks "*Who do people say that I Am?*" His disciples give Him several answers. "*Some say John the Baptist. Some say Elijah, and others Jeremiah or one of the prophets.*" Jesus then asks, "*But, Who do you say I Am?*"

We must answer that question correctly because there are a lot of varied answers. Many say Jesus is a god, a prophet, teacher, leader, good man, role model. Progressive "christians" and deconstructionists teach about a Jesus that is not from the Bible. Perennialists and panentheists teach Jesus is not Christ, but that Christ is bigger than Jesus, that Christ is in everything *as* everything. Christ is in the garbage *as* the garbage? Where are they getting this garbage? Definitely not from the Bible.

Who is Jesus? This is the most critical question of all, because the answer to this question answers all the other significant questions. Answering the question, "*Who is Jesus?*" correctly will let us know the meaning of life. Answering the question, "*Who is Jesus?*" correctly will let us know why we are here, that there is a God, what happens when we die, that there is a heaven and a hell, and that there is absolute truth. And answering this question, "*Who is Jesus?*" correctly is pointing them to Jesus in the Bible.

A Compelling Vision

When I am given the responsibility and honour to teach or preach, I put myself in the place of the hearers who may be new to it all and would be asking the preacher, *"Why? Why should I do these things you are preaching, Preacher? What should motivate me to do this and not do that? Because it is commanded? So "just do it?" Just stoicism?"* Yes, we are to obey All and Only as God commands, but more than just dutifully. Because then we will all just do or not do out of guilt or fear for not doing or doing. Or we will just do or not do out of pride for doing and not doing. Do you need to read that over? To put it another way, we should not be motivated by guilt, fear, or pride. We need a compelling reason and vision why.

When our children were younger and did not yet understand or know it all, they must simply obey our instruction. As they matured, we gave instruction and helped them understand why because we will not be around forever, and they will need to make wise decisions on their own. We gave instruction and why so that they will have the compelling reason and vision to motivate their decisions on their own.

This is important. People need to see Jesus, know Jesus, love Jesus, and hunger for Jesus *before* they will even think of hastening His return. We cannot simply tell people, *"Hasten The Wedding!"* I mean, we can, but they really need to have a compelling reason and vision why, why hasten His return? Why hasten the Wedding?

At the end of my teachings and preachings, I always try to show them Jesus in the text because all of The Word is about Him and points to Him (John 5:39). I am a happy *"doorkeeper in the house of the Lord"* (Psalm 84:10 ESV) stepping aside so people can see Him, not me. With the power of the Holy Spirit, I try my best to help them see how beautiful and magnificent Jesus really is, help them fall in love with Him, and take them to The Fountain so their thirsty souls can drink! As they meet with Jesus and drink from The Fountain, their cup cannot help but be filled to overflowing and overflowing to others.

Water to Wine

Near the end of 2020, we knew our time in the States was drawing down to under two years. We began to pray and ask God to *"teach us to number our days that we may get a heart of wisdom,"* (Psalm 90:12 ESV) and how to *"make the best use of the time"* (Ephesians 5:16 ESV).

John 2 is when Jesus is with His disciples at a wedding in Cana. The old wine has run out, and Jesus tells the servants to fill the vessels with water, which He then turns into new wine, the good wine (ESV), the best wine (NLT).

Around Christmas or New Year, I had a dream where I saw the large vessels that were empty of the old wine. Jesus was saying to fill the vessels with "water," and *He will* bring the new wine, the good wine, the best wine. When I looked closer, the vessels had names on them—the names of our children and folks we are discipling. But some of the vessels had no names. *"Not yet,"* God said. Those vessels represent the people for whom we have been praying, those into whom we would be pouring what has been poured into us.

Since 2013, my relationship with my #1 son, my eldest son, Runner, has been no more than just polite. For his own reasons, he decided that he could not spend any more time with me, and so began seven long years of painful silence and avoidance from him. But God, being rich in grace and mercy, has miraculously restored our relationship to where we see or at least talk to each other almost every other day. Robbi and I are still beside ourselves with amazement! What joy it is to pour into him all that Jesus has taught me and is teaching me. I have the privilege to disciple my firstborn son again! It is so good to see him *"hold fast to the Word of Life"* (Philippians 2:16 ESV) and run the race holding fast his eyes on Jesus! (Hebrews 12:2) And while bedridden in my covid room last month, Runner was *The*

Man—managing our company and visiting me every day at the hospital and Robbi at home. Have I mentioned how good God is to me?!

Bob Noyes, whom I introduced to you in Chapter 7, said of me, *"I would rather tame a wild mustang than kick a dead horse to life."*

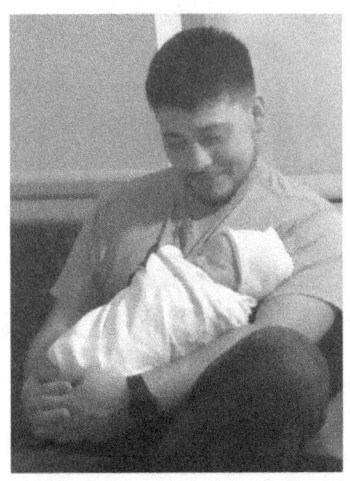

Nathaniel is a young man whom I love as a son, as Paul loved Timothy. I shared with Nate what Bob said to me because he was also ruffling the feathers of others [IMAGE 10] whose knickers were getting all bunched up and uncomfortable. Taming this wild mustang was a joy-filled ride—working together every day to partnering in missions to the other side of the world, to even simple pleasures such as Steak-Umm sandwiches every Friday night after (PBR) Public Bible Reading and prayer. I am so excited writing this today because, after almost ten months of praying due to a pause from Nathaniel, I believe God is restoring and will again allow me the privilege and joy to pour into this vessel. You see, God Himself has been taming this young mustang as He is still taming me, the wildest OG mustang. Thank God for His patience in the slow sanctification of Antonio Raul.

I can only give all thanks to God! Praise Him that in spite of all that transpired with my family, my relationship with my son Harrison has weathered it, though not perfectly. We have had our struggles because I am an imperfect Dad. What a joy it was to see him go on missions on his own to Uganda and then for him to partner with us in the Philippines, where the children of Gun-Ob squatter village flocked to him like the Pied Piper. They adored him! It is only by God's amazing grace and mercy that Harrison and I have a strong relationship. I am truly blessed by God that I may continue to disciple and pour into him, that is, when he is not too busy. It is a joy to see him reaching out and pouring into his friends what is being poured into him. Atta boy, Bubz!

Have I mentioned Micah, the son-in-law whom I love most? Very proud of this young man who is passionately pursuing God and all and only what God has for him as He leads him. Understandably busy caring for my daughter and the four most precious and beautiful grandbabies in the history of the world, managing his thriving company, Mighty Hand Construction, and pastoring folks, we try to get together as much as we can. While it is not often, our meetings are very intentional and full as we do not bother with superficialities. We dive headfirst into the deep waters of Jesus and His Word and His work in us and the world. I absolutely love pouring into this young man of God!

Besides her steadfast love and desire for Jesus and more of Him, and other than her *"imperishable beauty of a gentle and quiet spirit, which in God's sight is very precious"* (1 Peter 3:4 ESV), one of the most attractive things about Robbi Gail is how she pours out her life for the gals she disciples. She would attest to the same joys as she faithfully and firmly pours into Sarah, Hannah, Jeanine, and the gals of her Bible study. She so deeply cares for them and desires only God's best for them, which is Himself.

We are being obedient to God and filling these and other vessels with "water," as we trust we have heard Him. And Jesus is the One Who will turn the "water" into good wine, the best wine!

What is this "water" we are pouring into these vessels? We come to the Fountain of living waters (Jeremiah 2) and drink our fill. Jesus says, *"The water that I will give him will become in him a spring of living water welling up to eternal life."* Our cup will be overflowing (Psalm 23) into these vessels, into our children, and into the men and women we disciple. *Jesus* will bring new wine!

We are and will be pouring out Jesus as the living water, teaching and pouring into them all we have learned and what has been poured into us. We will also teach and always encourage them to go themselves to the Fountain of living waters to drink—Jesus Time. As Jesus was implying to the man *"who had been an invalid for 38 years"* (John 5:5 ESV) and waiting by the Bethesda pool, we tell them, *"You do not need that pool. It is a broken cistern. You need only Jesus. Go to the Fountain for yourself and drink."*

"Turn your eyes upon Jesus. Look full in His wonderful face And the things of earth will grow strangely dim..." (Helen H. Lemmel).[64]

No one else and nothing else will ever satisfy or quench our thirsty souls.

A Portrait of Jesus

We are nearing the end of our journey in this book. Before I let down my landing gear, we are going to cruise for a moment to even higher altitudes to give you a compelling vision and portrait of our beautiful God and Saviour, Jesus Christ.

As an obedient and faithful doorkeeper, I shall step aside now. Let us turn our eyes upon Him.

See yourself following a crowd to the wilderness of Judea to see a man wearing camel-hair clothing with a pouch full of locusts. A wild man whom hundreds of people are going to see to be baptized in the Jordan River. He sticks his hand in his bag to grab a bite for his lunch. Do you see him? Do you see the crowd?

One day, you see another One approach, and the locust man points Him out to the crowd. This One is different. You hear that they are having a little discussion, almost a debate. It seems the One is trying to convince him to baptize Him, but the camel hair dude is hesitant. Finally, he is persuaded and proceeds to baptize Him. When He comes up out of the water, you and the hundreds with you witness the clouds and heavens part, and all of you hear God the Father's thundering yet gentle voice, *"THIS is my beloved Son, in Whom I Am well-pleased."* And You see God the Holy Spirit coming down on Him and then leading Him into the wilderness.

Sometime later, you see this One Whom God calls His Son walking along the sea of Galilee. You are there fishing because that is what you do. There are a bunch of you there working, catching fish and handling fish, and smelling very much like fish.

He calls out to you in Aramaic, "*Deute opizo.*"

And you say, "*Huh?*"

He says to you, "*Come and follow Me. Turn away from your old life, your old self. Die to it actually. Come away with Me. Come and walk with Me awhile. Come and learn from Me. Come and watch Me. Come and watch Me teach. Come and watch Me heal and do miracles. Come and watch Me feed and care for people. Come and watch Me love the unlovely and the unloved and the hard-to-love. Come and eat with Me. Come and be with me. I know you smell like fish and are dirty. You don't have to clean yourself. You don't have to do anything. There will be time for doing. There will be a lot to do. But there will be time enough for that. Right now, just come and hang with Me. Come and know Me. Come and understand what I Am all about. Come and spend time with Me...*

So, you follow Him. You see Him teach and feed people. You see Him miraculously heal a leper, a blind man, a paralytic. You see the demons obey Him when He casts them out of people. You see Him calm a frightening storm and the roaring sea. You see Him raise a man called Lazarus from the dead who has been in the tomb 4 days! You hear Him declare that He is The Christ and that He is God. After all you have witnessed, there is no room for doubt.

But then He tells you...

"*I Am going to suffer. I Am going to the Cross to be crucified and give My Life in your place, pouring out My Blood to pay all your sin and debt, completely complete, to become the anger appeasement that will fully satisfy the justice and wrath of God against you, that you might become My righteousness, perfectly perfect, and be reconciled to God. Yes, I will die, and I will be buried, but...*

I will rise and live again on the third day! Count on it.

Then I will ascend into Heaven, and the Holy Spirit will come to comfort you, help you, and guide you. He will dwell in you and give you power to be My ambassador-witnesses to the ends of the earth for this mission: go and make disciples of every people group. This is my last command before I ascend to My Father. Reach the nations!

*When you make disciples of every people group and have taught them all that I have commanded you, **THEN** I shall return. I will come to rule and reign. I will redeem all of this old creation into a new creation and save the nations and establish justice and righteousness forever and ever and ever!*

And I will come back for you. I will say to you, "well done." But more importantly, far more significantly than patting you on the back for all your good work because it is not really about what you do, I will then say to you as I first called you… 'Enter into My Joy! Come away with Me. Let's have The Wedding now, the Joy of all joys! Spend eternity with Me, my Beloved.'"

He who testifies to these things says, "Surely I Am coming soon." Amen. Come, Lord Jesus! (Revelations 22:20 ESV).

"Does this set your heart to beating faster? Are you really in love with Him, or do you have a dead religion that is quite meaningless? Oh, my friend, Christ is so wonderful! Simon Peter loved Him. Paul loved Him, and all of those who have genuinely served Him have loved Him. I hope you love Him today" (J. Vernon McGee).[65]

Christ is so wonderful. I pray you love Him today.

Practical Application Questions:

1. What did you learn about Jesus? How does it draw you closer to Him?

_____

_____

_____

_____

_____

2. What is the difference between wanting to hear Him say, *"Well done, good and faithful servant,"* and *"Enter into My joy for eternity."*?

_____

_____

_____

_____

_____

3. Read Luke 10:38-42. How would you describe your relationship with Jesus? *"Distracted with much serving"* 10:39 ESV)? Or *"sitting at His feet and listening to His teaching"* (10:38)?

_____

_____

_____

_____

Choose the Better Thing

Luke 10 tells us the story of two sisters, Mary and Martha, who were with Jesus. More than the story is the deeper lesson Jesus teaches us to choose the better thing. I will not delve long into this as I want you to still have that picture of Jesus calling you and inviting you to spend today and eternity with Him. This is the better thing—to be with Him. Please choose the better thing.

Back in Chapter 3, I told you about my friend, David Lewin. I had the joy of working with David, driving around in a small black Ranger serving dealerships from Colorado to Wyoming every week. During those long drives, we would listen to and relish the teachings from Piper and Keller. I also had the privilege of worshiping and leading worship with him for several churches and 24-hour worship conferences. We played and prayed together—frisbee Taps and frisbee football, prayer nights and weekends. I had the honour to pour into David about my Jesus-times, portraits of Jesus, and all the stuff and ramblings he endured that are now this book that you are holding.

David is a profoundly gifted worship leader—a true Doxologist. For the last Song for Reflective Worship, I want to share with you the song written by David, "*I Choose the Better Thing*." May these words move you to choose the better thing and stir up a hunger for Jesus and a longing for His return.

Pick a verse or ten to memorize this week to hear God's voice.

Pray these verses back to God.

Sing to Him a song of reflective worship.

SONG FOR REFLECTIVE WORSHIP
Choose the Better Thing by David Lewin[66]

"So quickly I forget the joy that I can find
when I spend time with You
With life and all its demands at a hundred miles an hour
My days are up and down depending on what I have to do
But when I wake up in the morning, I am still with You
I am still with You

And I choose the better thing
I choose to sit at Your feet
I choose the better thing
To be with You, to be with You

How quickly I forget that I'm only where I am because
of Your hand
With life and all its surprises within Your sovereign plan
I see the wicked prosper in what they find to do
But when I enter the house of my God
There's nothing besides You, nothing but You

So, I choose the better thing
I choose to sit at Your feet
I choose the better thing
To be with You, to be with You…"

PRAYER JOURNAL

_____

_____

_____

_____

_____

_____

_____

_____

_____

_____

_____

_____

_____

_____

_____

_____

_____

_____

_____

_____

_____

11. *LANDING*

I will land here by being humbly honest. Who knows how many copies of this book will sell or even if it will sell at all? For sure, I should be able to count on my family to buy at least one or two, I think. Probably. Positive. Kinda.

Truthfully, this does not have to be a bestseller. This does not have to sell thousands or even hundreds of copies.

What matters most is not the sales of this book but the fruit of it. If only a small group of people take this and run with it, if only handfuls read this and apply it, really, if only twelve people resolve to let Jesus do His job and they do theirs of going and making disciples, that is probably enough to see Jesus return in this generation. That is my highest *and* greatest *and* ultimate goal and motivation for everything I do, say, write, preach or teach. Nothing and no one will make me happier than to see my Lord face to face and be with Him for eternity!

I have good friends who tell me that they too want to see Jesus, but first, they want to see their children grow up. I get it. I would love to watch my grandkids grow up! Nothing wrong with that. But, if we want *that* more than seeing Jesus, then that means we love that more than we love Him. And if we love anything more than God, then we are not loving Him with all of our heart, all of our soul, all of our strength and all of our mind.

Sadly, this is the testimony we hear from most Christians. "*As much as I love my God, I am in no hurry to reach heaven.*" Well, I am in a hurry to see heaven, or more accurately, to see Jesus. But I do not have a death wish, nor am I in a hurry to die. I just want to see Jesus.

When we all get to heaven,
What a day of rejoicing that will be!
When we all see Jesus,
We'll sing and shout the victory!
Eliza E. Hewitt[67]

See, folks, I know I will see Jesus when I die. I pray that I see Him *before* then! The real question is... do you? If not, then you need to ask yourself:

"Where am I finding my greatest joy?

_____

_____

_____

_____

_____

My highest fulfillment?

_____

_____

_____

_____

My deepest satisfaction?

_____

_____

_____

_____

My truest happiness?"

_____

_____

_____

_____

_____

Let me encourage you to walk through the Gospels of Jesus again. Slowly. Do not take a quick shower, but bathe in His Word. Immerse yourself in It and be saturated. Let your soul drink, drink deep at The Fountain. Dust off His portrait and gaze long upon His beauty. Let His face be clear in your eyes, engraved on your heart, and ignite your soul!

"And the Lord answered me: "Write the vision; make it plain on tablets, so he may run who reads it" (Habakkuk 2:2 ESV).

Friends, our task is doable and finishable. We can reach the nations, all the unreached nations. We have more than enough resources to do it. We can see Jesus sooner than later. We can hasten The Wedding—the Joy of all joys!

"Amen. Come, Lord Jesus" (Revelations 22:20 ESV).

"Now you are light in the Lord. Walk as children of light" (Ephesians 5:8 ESV), *"blameless and innocent, children of God without blemish in the midst of a crooked and twisted generation, among whom you shine as lights in the world"* (Philippians 2:15 ESV), *"that you may proclaim the excellencies of Him Who called you out of darkness into His marvelous light"* (1 Peter 2:9 ESV). Lights are not meant to light up a place that is already lit. Lights are meant to go where it is dark and needing light. They are meant to light up the darkness. Go light it up!

Now. Turn all this knowledge into "shoe leather" and walk it, run it, and live it. Shine! And go make disciples of all people groups!

12. DISCIPLESHIP STORIES and ECHOES OF HEAVEN

"One of my favorite memories is living on Koenigstein Avenue because we lived across the street from the Davy family and being able to see them almost every day. This was genuine Acts 2-Church with both of our families and everybody and their sister's neighbor's nephew's professor's students and families! I relished the frequent talks and worship and prayer with my very good friend, Tim. Constantly bringing him new songs for him to biblically critique. Basketball and movies and games and pouring into his boys, Ben and Jesse and Zach who came over like... A LOT! And they had many opportunities to observe my not-always-perfect Christian life. I remember telling my little sister Michel that there were only a few guys I would love to see her marry, to which she responded, "He's just a kid!* (referring to Jesse). *But... she did end up marrying the kid!* "25 summers ago." *What a joy to have discipled Jesse when he was just a kid, a teen and into a godly man and to see the fruit of it in my sister, my handsome nephew and his beautiful sisters."* (kuya raul)

*"I've learned over the past few years that truly kindred spirits in this life are a very rare commodity and that I consider you to be just that, and I love you. In some ways I had imagined the best of that as yet to be, but what we've had up to now has been wonderful, and who knows what the future may hold. I'm always amazed at the experience (which I've had over and over in my life) of having someone be a 'routine' part of my life, settling into the thought that it will always be seasons. Maybe that's the best way to put it; knowing your friendship has been an **'echo of heaven'** and that's probably the best we can do for one another this side of there... Let us press on together, in obedience, to do all we can to 'hasten the day.'* (tim)

"The love, respect, and appreciation I have for you fails to express with words. If words could express how I feel when I say thank you...let it be so. Thank you! I thank God for having

our paths cross. It's a blessing to work under you, to worship beside you, and to pray together with you. ... I'm grateful to have someone so loving and caring in my life. Thank you for both your support and your wife to come alongside us! We love and appreciate you guys both so very much!" (nathaniel)

"My favorite part of 'Taps' was how excited you were to play it. I'm still not very good with frisbee. Great memories from the Forerunners trip. I am grateful for everyone... You and Glenn have made great investments in our lives. You sometimes asked for more than we thought possible. You brought harmony out of our crackling voices and appreciation for order in our performance. Thank you for teaching us meaning in the responsibility God allows us to carry. I'm praying for God's blessing on your work and looking forward to reading soon." (christian)

"I heard from other people how they felt like they were no more than just another notch on someone's spiritual belt, just another rung climbing the "Christian ladder." What I truly loved and appreciated about being discipled was that she never made me feel like that. I was not just another project to her. We were not moving along on her timeline and agenda, but she waited on God's leading. It was real. It was very genuine." (missy)

"People right away assume I have the gift of prophecy because of my passion to speak and preach the truth, but sadly not always in love or with gentleness. My "excuse" always was that I did not have the gift of mercy. And as I was meeting with my discipler, Mark Stortvedt, I told him that I would just say to people, "You want mercy? Go to Jesus." Mark leaned across the table, looked me directly in my eyes, and gently said, "But Jesus lives in you." Ouch. (kuya raul)

"Just came back from a discipleship meeting with a young man. We talked a lot about his struggles with laziness, lack of consistency in the Word, to his struggles with lust. Not much different than any other young man, or even older men for that matter. We looked and talked through Scripture and prayed, but bottom-line,

175

the remedy for his struggle was his desperate need to see his desperate need for Jesus, "for He stands at the right hand of the needy one," (Psalm 109:31). All of us are the needy one. When we see our need, our desperate need, then we shall see that God is with us, at our right hand." (tony)

"When I was 16 years old, Jim Carlson took the time to disciple me, despite being your typical 16-year-old with the typical 16-year-old mentality and attitude and orneriness. With incredible patience, he helped me grow as a Christian and then even took me on a mission trip to the Philippines! What really still stands out is that he took the time for me. (kevin)

"Discipleship is life-on-life—inviting others to come and share your life and watch your life. Back in Jersey when I first started in "official" ministry, I did what my discipler did with me and what I read and saw in the Scriptures. I invited the youth and young adults to come and hang out with me. It still baffles me to this day that parents allowed their teens to leave their safe and comfortable suburbs to go with me to the non-touristy sections and streets of New York City. What was even crazier still is sometimes I would invite them at 11pm. And with no definite plan of when we might be back. Sometimes it would not be till 3 or 4am! Now, if a young man were to ask my own kids to go with them to Denver (which is far unlike NYC) around midnight, I would say they were nuts and do not know what they were asking! But, I guess these parents really trusted God with their kids with me as we worshipped in the car, walked around the city, saw and met all sorts of folks, prayed for some, and enjoyed the best Chinese food at Wo Hops!" (kuya raul)

"I met the Franciscos fairly early on in my walk with Jesus. I was overwhelmed by their heart not only for God, but for people. I was in a transitional stage of my life. I was raising 2 girls on my own, earning a wage of $15.40 per hour, paying every bill by myself, completely dependent on Jesus for each and every day. God says in Psalm 68:6 God sets the <u>lonely</u> in families." See, I was the lonely and God placed me with a family–The Franciscos. So, here I was, a single mom, with my $500 car in need of repair

as it would leak rain and snow from the roof. An opportunity came knocking on my door for a new job that could have the potential to change my circumstances drastically. But my vehicle was unreliable. I knew that I couldn't take that job unless I could get into another vehicle. Not only did I need a vehicle, but I needed dress shoes for my interview. Immediately, Robbi asked without hesitation, "What size shoe do you wear?" "8.5," I said. She happened to be the same size. Then almost in the same sentence she said, "Use my car until yours is fixed, no matter how long. It's not my car anyways, it's His, and by His, I mean God's." I could go on and on with examples of how the Franciscos exemplify Koinonia. I have been forever changed by their example. They bring whatever they have to the table, to serve others. It's interesting because about a year later after obtaining that new job, I actually had two cars and came across an opportunity to extend koinonia to another brother who was in need of a vehicle for about 6 weeks. The old Sarah would have been like, "What if he wrecks it? doesn't bring it back?" But because of (being discipled by Robbi) *without hesitation, I said, "Here take my car, please. It's not mine anyways... It's HIS."*

"Happy Birthday to one of the best mentors (discipler) *I have ever had! Robbi, thank you for living your life in a way that teaches better than any seminary school ever could... You are vital to the Kingdom of God!"* (sarah)

"I was meeting with a guy and talking about his debt and work (because finances and vocation are part of discipleship). There was an issue of working a particular night when he could earn some money to pay off debt in which he is very behind. Or he could not work and go to prayer that night. Does God instruct us to not be in debt in His Word? Does God command us in His Word to be part of a Prayer Group on specific nights?" It is clear from God's Word that we are to work and pay our debts. It is also clear from God's Word that we pray together and pray always. But it is not clear from God's Word that we pray on Thursday night from 6-8pm. 'Specific' weeknight prayer meetings, while good, are actually not found in Scripture, otherwise people would be in sin if they do not attend." (reg)

"Discipling a young husband and father. He was excited about a weekly evening meeting after his work to meet with a couple unbelievers to discuss the Bible. Awesome! But he also talked about neglecting his responsibilities to care for his wife and children and he knew he needed to make time for them. God commands us to care for our wives and children. To nurture them. To disciple them. To wash them with the Word. But does He command us to meet with pre-believers on a scheduled weekly night to evangelize them? We are commanded to love our families and evangelize but manage our own households well first (1 Timothy 3:5). Do not do the second, if the first is neglected." (rbf)

"You have been the one to help me grasp the faith and to grow in the love of Christ for several years, and you discipled me also through the hard times without growing weary of the task." (peter)

"When we were starting the College Group, I started calling all the numbers on the list given to me from the church office. One particular number, I called and asked for Jose. The guy who answered said Jose was no longer in that dorm room and did not know where he was. So, I asked him his name, which was Neil. Then I asked him, "Hey, Neil! What are you doing tonight? Wanna come over for our College Group?" Neil did come over. And he kept coming over, almost every night! I can still remember him bringing Quarter Pounders with cheese and Big Mac Sauce every Sunday night after our Sud Z (Sunday Life) meetings and he would just hang out till who knows when because everyone knew our house was open 25 hours a day!" (kuya raul)

"I was in a deep state of depression to the point where I doubted God's love for me. It came to the point where I felt that my only option was admitting myself to a hospital. There was no one I could contact, and I did not feel safe driving myself there. The Lord put Robbi on my heart. She picked me up, and I asked her to drive me to a hospital. Instead, she took me to her own home and said, 'You don't need a hospital; you need Jesus.' For the next two weeks, Robbi and Antonio took me in as their own daughter. Despite the way I had turned away from God, they loved me as

Jesus loves me and showed me His grace and forgiveness. Robbi nurtured and discipled me through some of the darkest moments of my life. She took me under her wing in discipleship and poured His Word into my heart, showing me the truth of Who He is and what Jesus did for me by dying on the cross. Throughout each day, Robbi and I read Scriptures together, prayed together, and worshiped together. When I couldn't sleep, she stayed up all night with me and constantly reminded me of Jesus' unconditional, irrevocable love for me, despite what

I believed of myself. The Lord worked through Robbi and Antonio to make an incredible impact on my life and my walk with God through discipleship. As they served the Lord, my life was changed and is still being changed to this day." (hannah)

RESOURCES and ENDNOTES

Suggested Reading

Hunger for God by John Piper

We Would See Jesus by Roy Hession

Letters to The Church by Francis Chan

The Master Plan of Evangelism by Robert Coleman

Multiply by Francis Chan

Until Unity by Francis Chan

The End For Which God Created the World by Jonathan Edwards

The Gospel of the Kingdom by George Eldon Ladd

Thirty Years That Changed The World by Michael Green

ENDNOTES

1   Green, Michael. Thirty Years That Changed the World. Grand Rapids, MI: Wm. B. Eerdman Publishing Co, 2002.

2   Merida, Tony. Christ-Centered Exposition Commentary: Exalting Jesus in Acts. Nashville, TN: B&H Publishing Group, 2017.

3   Coleman, Robert E. The Master Plan of Evangelism. Grand Rapids, MI: Revell, a division of Baker Publishing Group, 1993.

4   Chan, Francis and Mark Beuving. Multiply. Colorado Springs, CO: David C. Cook, 2012.

5   Crosby, Fanny. "Blessed Assurance." Public Domain,

6   Gaultiere, Bill. "Pastor Stress Statistics." Soul Shepherding, accessed August 13, 2021. https://www.soulshepherding.org/pastors-under-stress/

7   Krejcir, Richard J. "Statistics on Pastors." Into Thy Word. Francis A. Schaeffer Institute of Church Leadership Development, 2007. http://www.intothyword.org/apps/articles/?articleid=36562.

8   Van Auken, Phil. "Understanding Church Burnout and What to Do About It." Baylor University, accessed August 12, 2021. http://business.baylor.edu/Phil_VanAuken/ChurchBurnout.html

9   Ditchfield, Christin and Mary Jane. "Burned-Out Volunteers." Today's Christian Women. Christianity Today, 2007. https://www.todayschristianwoman.com/articles/2007/may/burned-out-volunteers.html

10 Rainer, Thom, S. "Five Common Reasons Church Members Burnout." Church Answers Featuring Thom Rainer, February 1, 2016. https://churchanswers.com/blog/five-common-reasons-church-members-burnout/

11 Hession, Roy and Revel Hession. We Would See Jesus: Discovering God's Provision for You in Christ. Fort Washington, PA: CLC Publications, 2019.

12 "Types/List of Christian Ministries." Disciple Christian. Accessed August 13, 2021. http://disciplechristian.com/types—lists-of-christian-ministries.html

13 Stedman, Ray C. Body Life: The Book That Inspired a Return to the Church's Real Meaning and Mission. Grand Rapids, MI: Our Daily Bread Publishing, 1972.

14 Wesley, Charles. "And Can It Be That I Should Gain." Public Domain, 1738.

15 Chan, Francis. Until Unity. Colorado Springs, CO: David C. Cook, 2021.

16 Robinson, Robert. "Come, Thou Fount of Every Blessing." Public Domain, 1758.

17 "Average Time Spent Daily on Social Media (Latest 2020 Data). BroadbandSearch.net, 2020. https://www.broadbandsearch.net/blog/average-daily-time-on-social-media

18 Robinson, Robert. "Come, Thou Fount of Every Blessing." Public Domain, 1758.

19 Cowper, William. "There is a Fountain Filled With Blood." Public Domain, 1772.

20 "How Should a Christian View Tradition?" Got Questions Ministries. April 26, 2021. https://www.gotquestions.org/Christian-tradition.html

21 Kranz, Jeffrey. "All the 'One Another' Commands in the NT [Infographic]." OverviewBible. March 9, 2014. https://overview-bible.com/one-another-infographic/

22 SAAN. "1050 New Testament Commands vs 613 Old Testament Commands, Which Do We Follow?" Christian Forums. February 24, 2014. https://www.christianforums.com/threads/1050-new-tes-tament-commands-vs-613-old-testament-commands-which-do-we-follow.7806880/#:~:text=1050%20NT%20Commands%201%20Sabbath%20began%20in%20Eden,TEN%20Commandments%20from%20Eden%20to%20this%20very%20day.

23 Piper, John. "How Do I Know If I'm Doing Enough for God?" Desiring God Foundation. July 20, 2020. https://www.desiringgod.org/interviews/how-do-i-know-if-im-doing-enough-for-god

24 Byrne, Mary E. and Eleanor H. Hull. "Be Thou My Vision." Public Domain, 1905.

25 HELPS Word-Studies from The Discovery Bible. Edited by Dr. Gleason Archer and Dr. Gary Hill. Helps Ministries Inc, Accessed April 9, 2021. https://thediscoverybible.com/

26 Piper, John. "All of Life as Worship." Desiring God. Desiring God Foundation. November 30, 1997. https://www.desiringgod.org/messages/all-of-life-as-worship

27 Ibid.

28 Coleman, Robert E. The Master Plan of Evangelism. Grand Rapids, MI: Revell, a division of Baker Publishing Group, 1993.

29 Crosby, Fanny. "Give Me Jesus." Public Domain, 1845.

30 Piper, John. "'I Will Build My Church' — From All Peoples." Desiring God. Desiring God Foundation, October 28, 2001. https://www.desiringgod.org/messages/i-will-build-my-church-from-all-peoples

31 Chan, Francis and Mark Beuving. Multiply. Colorado Springs, CO: David C. Cook, 2012.

32 Ibid.

33 Burroughs, F. G. "I Will Go." Public Domain, 1891.

34 Chan, Francis. Until Unity. Colorado Springs, CO: David C. Cook, 2021.

35 Coleman, Robert E. The Master Plan of Evangelism. Grand Rapids, MI: Revell, a division of Baker Publishing Group, 1993.

36 Bruce, Alexander Balmain. The Training of the Twelve. Kregel Publications, 1979.

37 Platt, David. "A Personal Disciple-Making Plan." Radical, May 29, 2017. https://radical.net/articles/a-personal-disciple-making-plan/

38 Keller, Timothy J. Sermon, New York, NY: Redeemer Presbyterian Church, 1994-1998.

39 Herr, M. L. "Full of Joy." Public Domain, 1896.

40 Klett, Leah MarieAnn. "Americans Spend More Money on Pet Halloween Costume Than Reaching the Lost: Missions Expert." The Christian Post. October 28, 2018 https://www.christianpost.com/news/americans-spend-more-money-pet-halloween-costumes-than-reaching-lost-missions-andrew-scott.html

41 PNW Conference. "How Churches Spend Their Money: 5 National Insights on Budget Priorities." Pacific Northwest Conference of The United Methodist Church. December 2, 2014. https://www.pnwumc.org/news/how-churches-spend-their-money/

42 Ramsey, Dave. Financial Peace: Restoring Financial Hope to You and Your Family. New York, NY: Viking Adult, 1997.

43 Chan, Francis. Letters to the Church. Colorado Springs, CO: David C. Cook, 2018.

44 Chan, Francis. Until Unity. Colorado Springs, CO: David C. Cook, 2021.

45 Ditzel, Peter. "The Worship Service and the New Testament Assembly, Part 2." Word of His Grace. 2017. https://www.wordofhis-grace.org/wp/worship-service/2/

46 Chan, Francis. Letters to the Church. Colorado Springs, CO: David C. Cook, 2018.

47 Chan, Francis. Until Unity. Colorado Springs, CO: David C. Cook, 2021.

48 Kuya Raul, "Bring Me Back To My First Love."

49 Spence-Jones, H. D. M., and Joseph. S. Excel. The Pulpit Commentary: 1 Thessalonians. Peabody, MA: Hendrickson Publishers, 1985.

50 Ibid.

51 Edwards, Jonathan. The End For Which God Created The World. Public Domain. 1765.

52 Lehman, Frederick Martin. "The Love of God." Public Domain, 1917.

53 Newton, John. "Amazing Grace." Public Domain, 1779.

54 Pascal, Frenchman Blaise. Pensées. Translated by John Walker. Public Domain, 1660/1688.

55 Tolstoy, Leo. Family Happiness. Translated by Louise and Aylmer Maude. Public Domain, 1859.

56 Edwards, Jonathan. The End For Which God Created The World. Public Domain. 1765.

57 Ladd, George Eldon. The Gospel of The Kingdom. Grand Rapids, MI: Wm. B. Eerdmans Publishing Co, 1959.

58 Ibid.

59 Coleman, Robert E. The Master Plan of Evangelism. Grand Rapids, MI: Revell, a division of Baker Publishing Group, 1993.

60 Chan, Francis and Danae Yankoski. Forgotten God: Reversing Our Tragic Neglect of the Holy Spirit. Colorado Springs, CO: David C. Cook. 2009.

61 Ibid.

62 Ibid.

63 Ackley, Alfred Henry. "His Love Is Far Better Than Gold." Public Domain, 1910.

64 Lemmel, Helen H. "Turn Your Eyes Upon Jesus." Public Domain, 1918.

65 McGee, J. Vernon. Thru The Bible Commentary. Nashville, TN: Thomas Nelson Inc. Publishers, 1984.

66 Lewin, David. "I Chose The Better Thing." David Lewin Music, 2013. https://davidlewinmusic1.bandcamp.com/

67 Hewitt, Eliza E. "When We All Get to Heaven." Public Domain, 1898.

COPYRIGHT PERMISSIONS:

187

Before we even see any sales for *"Why Simple Discipleship,"* any or all revenue is already predetermined to go toward 268Missions for His Name and renown to reach the unreached people groups of the Philippines and the 10/40 Window, all to hasten Jesus Christ our Bridegroom's return and The Wedding—the Joy of all joys! God bless your day.

Don't waste your life... INVEST YOUR LIFE!–YouTube

CPSIA information can be obtained
at www.ICGtesting.com
Printed in the USA
LVHW111936201021
700976LV00001B/51